SANDRA MUJINGA

CLOSED SPACE, OPEN WORLD

SOLO OSLO
MUNCH—2022

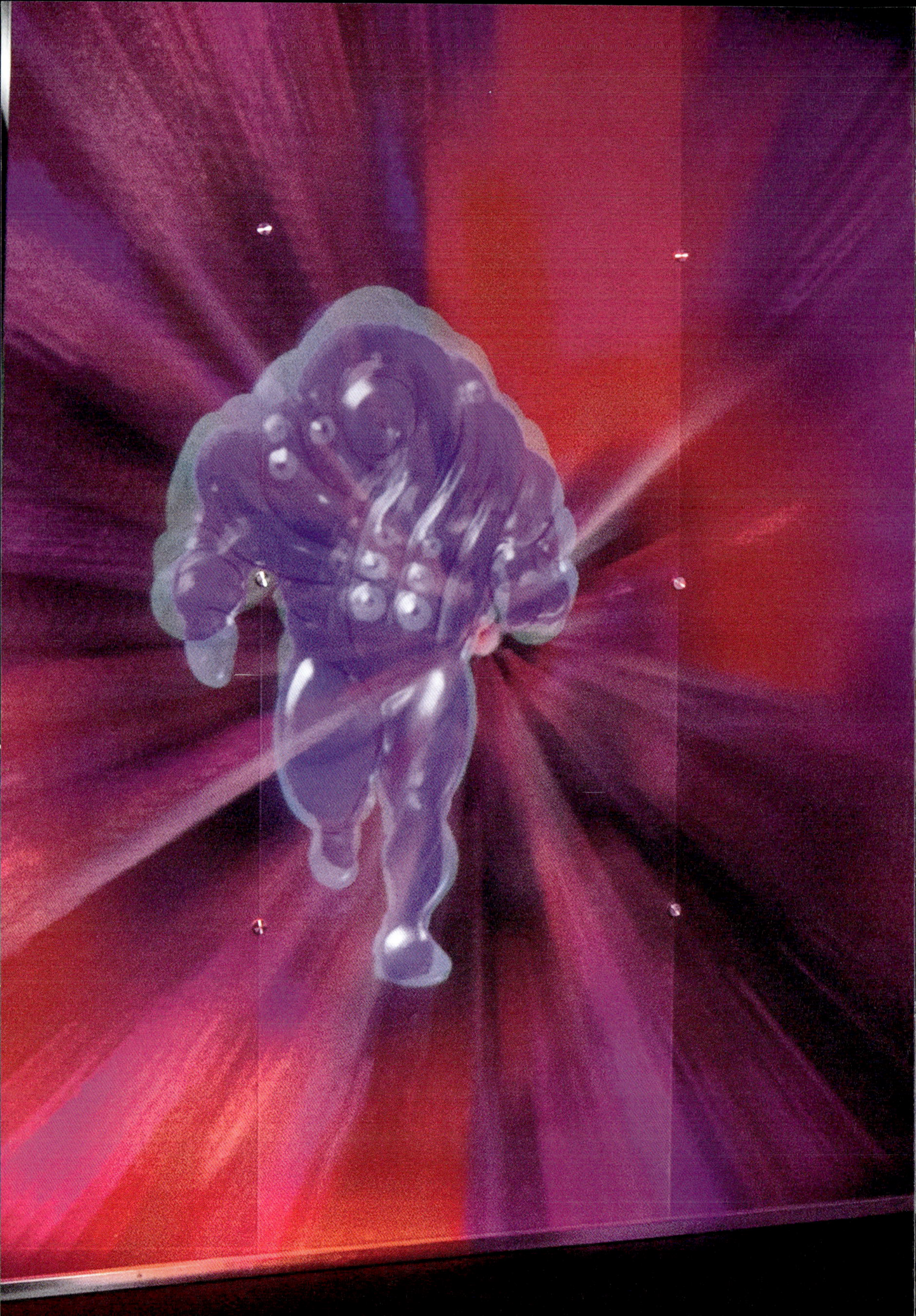

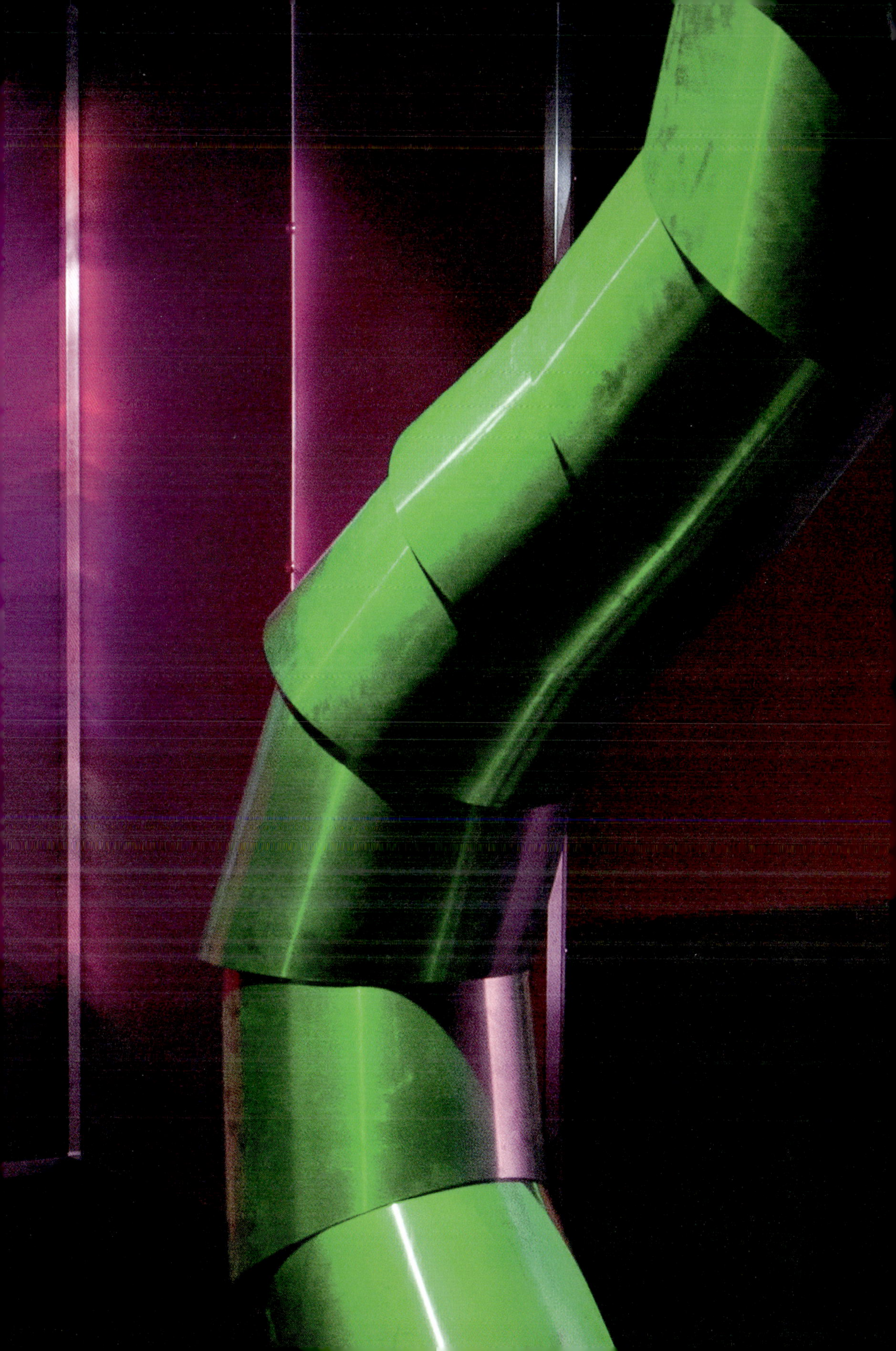

Tominga O'Donnell

SANDRA MUJINGA—

TOWARDS AN EXHIBITION HISTORY

I had not read much science fiction before my first conversation with Sandra Mujinga in 2019, but I have found that following an artist's literary recommendations offers a valuable point of entry to understanding their work. One author whose name kept coming up in our dialogue was N. K. Jemisin. In her book, *The Fifth Season*, an orogene is someone who can 'sess' earthquakes before they happen and use their extraordinary powers to absorb them, albeit at great physical cost. In a world devastated by natural disasters that usher in new 'seasons' the orogenes' strength is their ability to sense beyond the sensible, to notice seismic shifts before they turn into catastrophes. The figure of the orogene stayed with me as I tried to navigate Mujinga's rich and complex exhibition history leading up to her commission for MUNCH. It was particularly present as I watched Mujinga's performance, *You Are All You Need*, at her solo show at Bergen Kunsthall in 2019, in which two actors, Terese Mungai-Foyn and Mariama Ndure, ruminated on 'mourning the event by having exhibitions'. As audience members, we were not explicitly told what this 'event' had been, but its meaning was alluded to as the actors repeated their introductions to what initially seemed like a conventional 'artist talk', stating their names, where they were based and the mediums they worked in, before gradually providing more information. There were references to volcanic soil, to panic, to lava, to an eruption. One of them added, 'It could have been worse if we were next to the lake'. The actors' deadpan delivery could not mask the ominous sense of a disaster—past but also present. The story was located out of time and place. Ngogobeihli, where both artists were supposedly 'based', does not exist according to an internet search, although the name might be a reference to the Ngogo community of chimpanzees in Uganda.

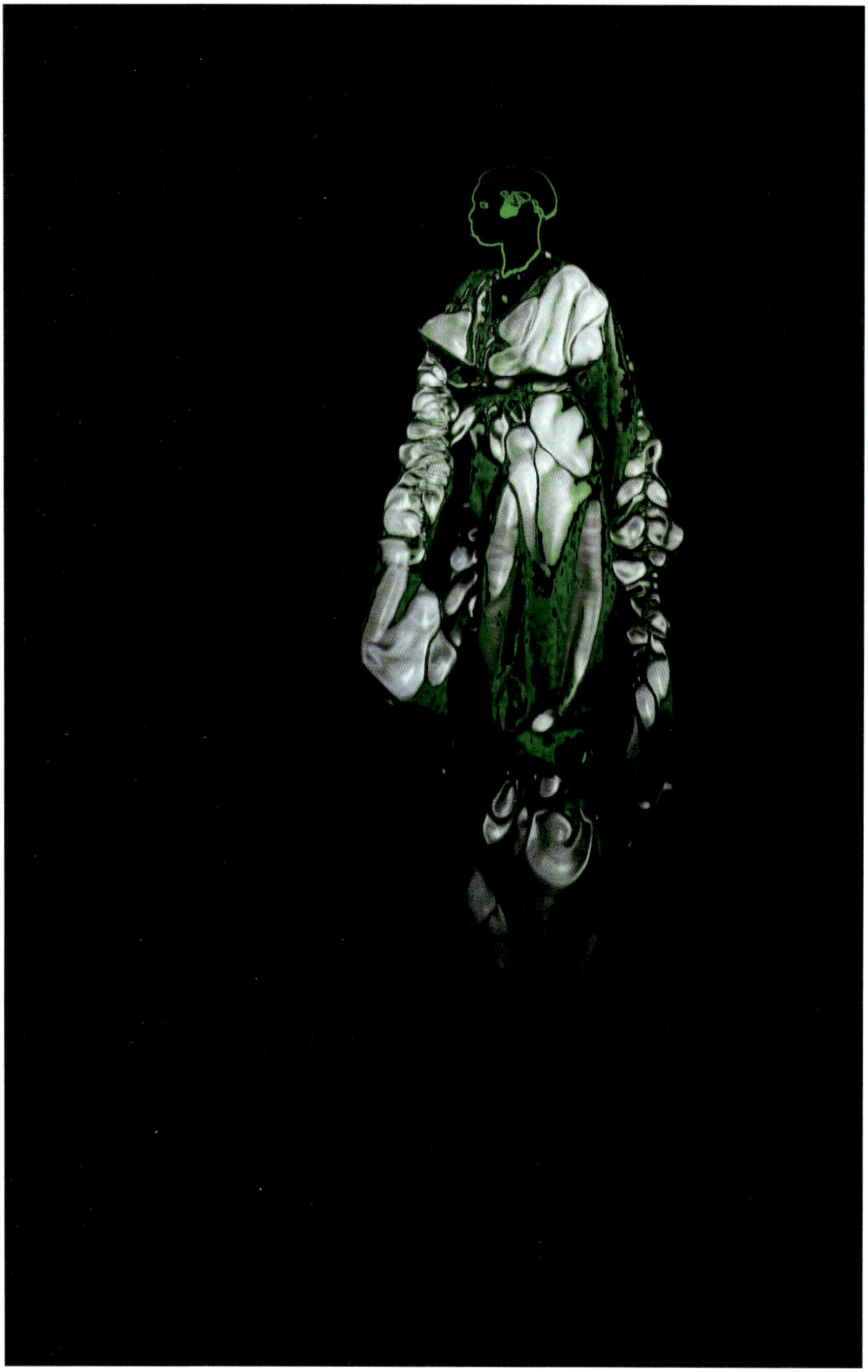

Sandra Mujinga, *Flo* (2019). Installation view from *SONW—Shadow of New Worlds* at Bergen Kunsthall. Photo: Thor Brødreskift.

By resemblance, the 'event' could refer to Mount Nyiragongo, an active stratovolcano in the Democratic Republic of Congo, just north of Lake Kivu and the town of Goma, Sandra Mujinga's place of birth. At the time of the performance, the volcano's last eruption was in 2002. It erupted again in 2021, causing mass panic, as the citizens of Goma had to evacuate quickly to avoid the imminent threat of flowing lava.

Opening at the end of 2019, Mujinga's solo exhibition in Bergen, entitled *SONW—Shadow of New Worlds*, featured two new works by the artist, including the centrepiece *Flo*—a video hologram, named after the artist's deceased mother. The eponymous character emerged, hovering in space, like some ethereal presence, before passing through a darkened corridor bisecting the largest gallery in the Kunsthall. The figure was outsized, a weightless giant with bulging muscles, draped in seagrass-like garments; the contours of its face and neck precisely drawn in profile in luminous green. 'Flo' might just as well have emerged from the depths below as the heavens above. The second new work in the exhibition, *Coiling*, drew on Mujinga's technique of combining artificial materials via their deconstruction: burnt acrylic paint, melted polyester and heat-treated PVC. *Coiling* resembled the tattered sails of a ghost ship or something found in the post-apocalyptic landscape of the mid-1980s sci-fi/ action film *Mad Max: Beyond Thunderdome.*

The exhibition in Bergen, billed as Mujinga's largest solo show to date, also included *Nokturnal Kinship* (2018), originally exhibited as part of her solo display *Calluses* at Tranen, outside Copenhagen. Large, hooded figures, pleather costumes with reflective detailing, hovered in the central gallery of the Kunsthall, bathed in the green light that has become a

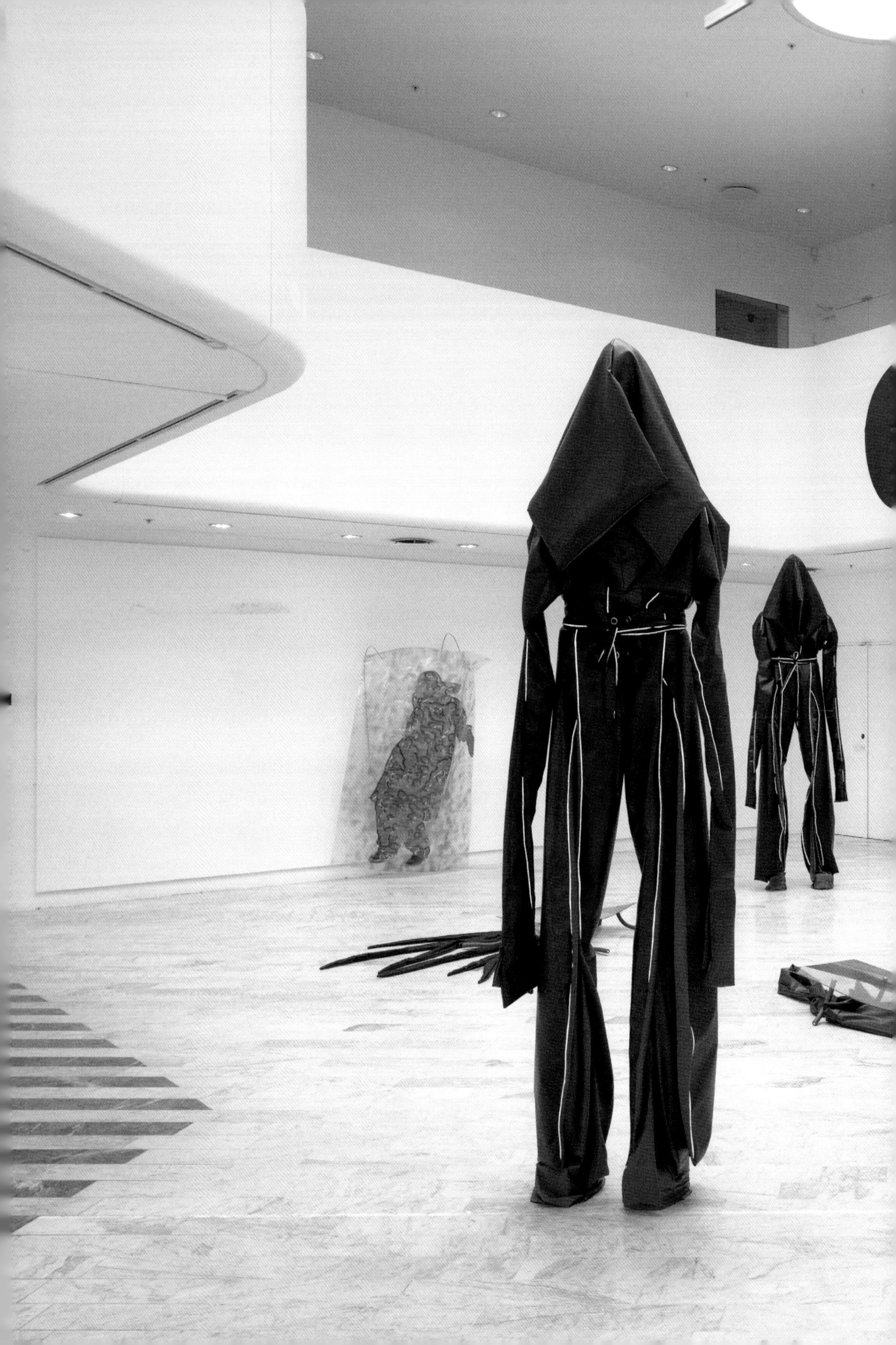

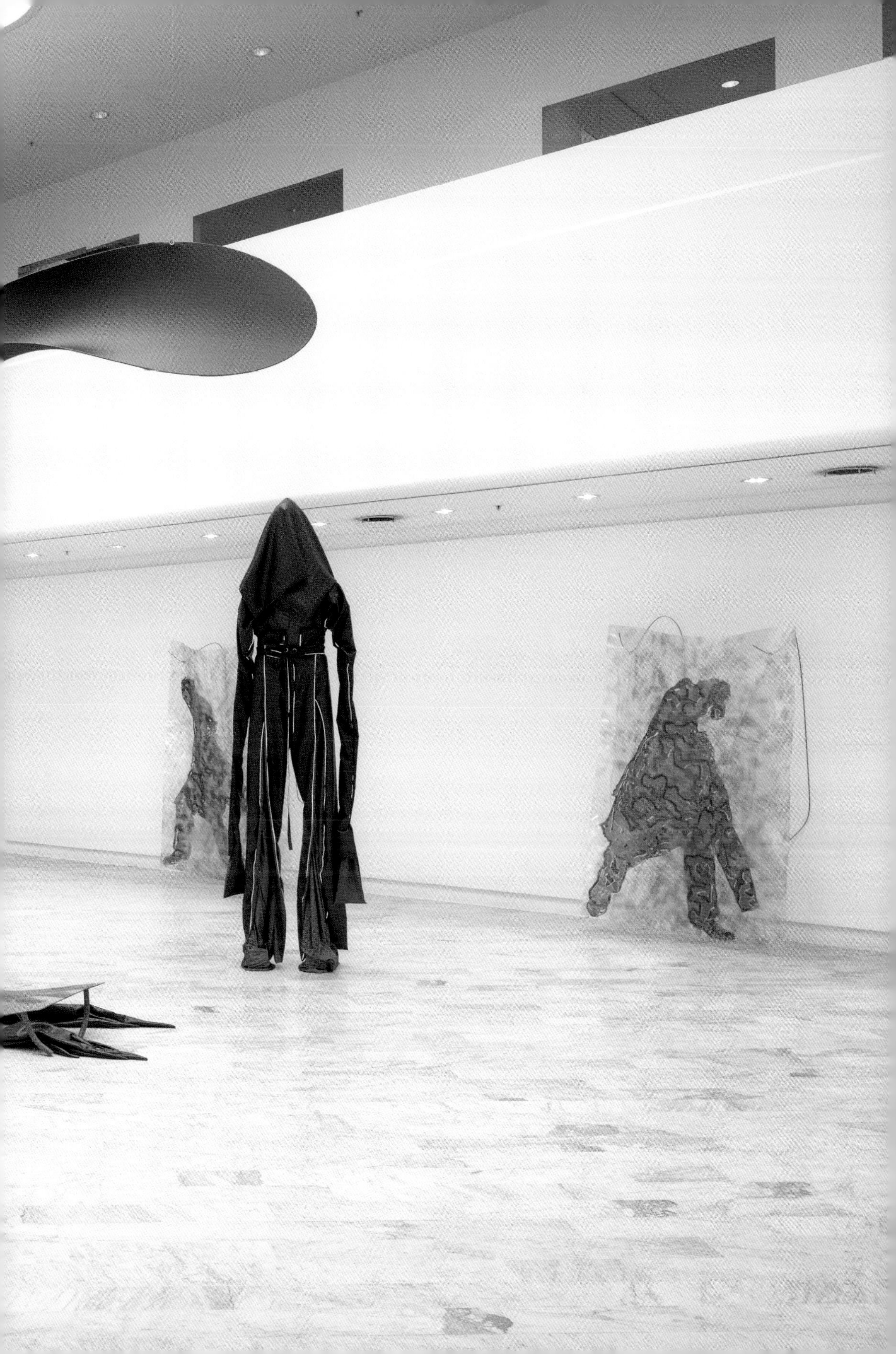

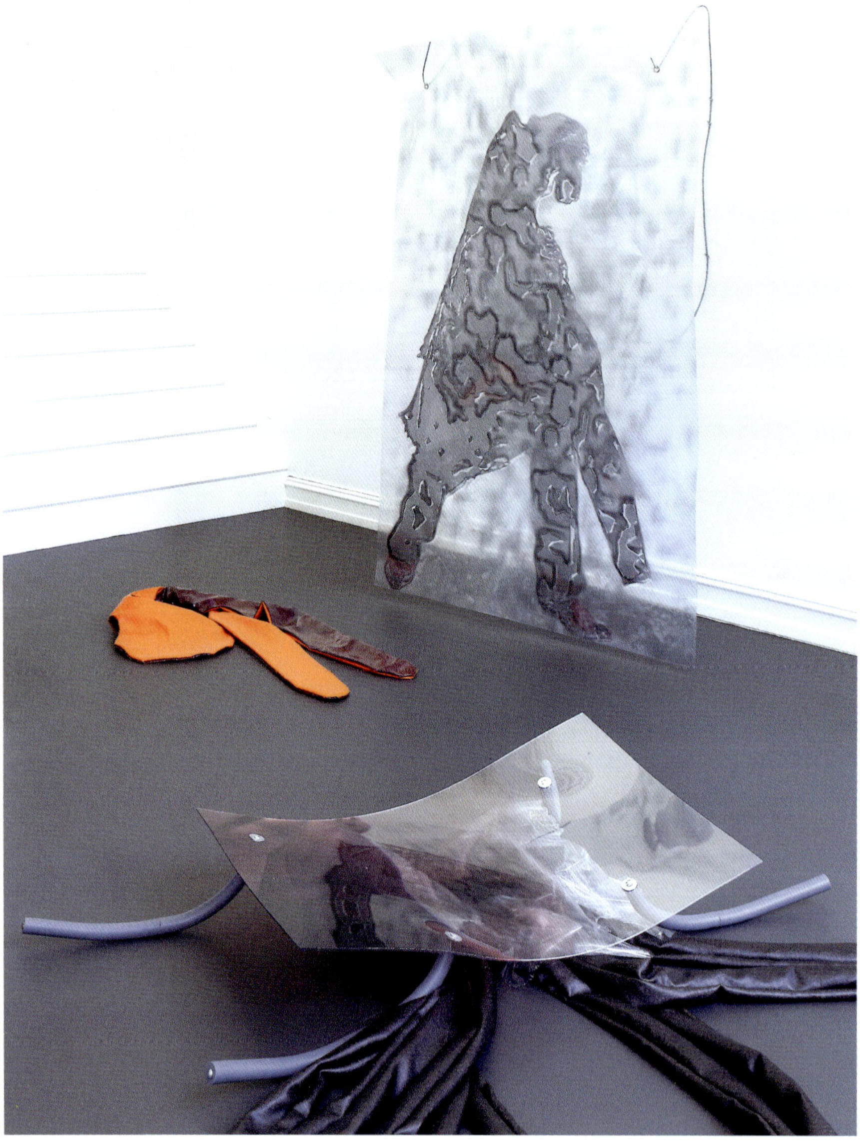

pp. 12—13 Sandra Mujinga, *Nokturnal Kinship* (2018). Installation view from *Calluses* at Tranen, Copenhagen. Nasjonalmuseet, Oslo.

Sandra Mujinga, *Camouflage Waves 1* (2018). Installation view from *Hoarse Globules* at UKS, Oslo. Photo by Jan Khür. Courtesy of the artist.

hallmark of Mujinga's installations. Another work, *Camouflage Waves 1—3* (2018), was previously shown at Tranen and in Mujinga's exhibition *Hoarse Globules* at the Young Artists' Society in Oslo. Here, standing figures—quite bulky as if dressed in oversized bomber jackets—were partially obscured from view by a semi-transparent covering made from inkjet print on film merged with soft PVC using heat. The degree of visibility varied, making it difficult to make out who or what was behind the surface layer, covered in viscous globs like raindrops on a windscreen. It generated a strong urge in me to wipe the screen, to uncover the hidden figure beneath or to reposition oneself so that the shape might emerge as human.

This denial of visibility runs through Mujinga's practice. It evokes the writer Édouard Glissant's concept of opacity, which he described in *Poetics of Relation* as a right one could demand: the right not to be understood. Drawing on his lived experience as a Martiniquan scholar based in France, Glissant formulated opacity as a strategy deployed against an expectation of transparency. It referred to the Other's right to reject the scrutiny and any claim of full comprehension, especially from Western colonial powers, though, as Glissant asserted, 'we clamour for the right to opacity for everyone'. At the opening of the 10th Berlin Biennale, entitled *We Don't Need Another Hero*, curator Gabi Ngcobo referred to Glissant as she launched the graphic identity of the biennial with camouflage as its guiding motif, claiming the right to opacity both on behalf of the works in the exhibition and herself as its presumed spokesperson. In a similar way in Mujinga's work, the opaque covering becomes the material manifestation of the titular camouflage. Another of the artist's works, the video *Disruptive Pattern* (2018), evoked a different kind of concealment, namely

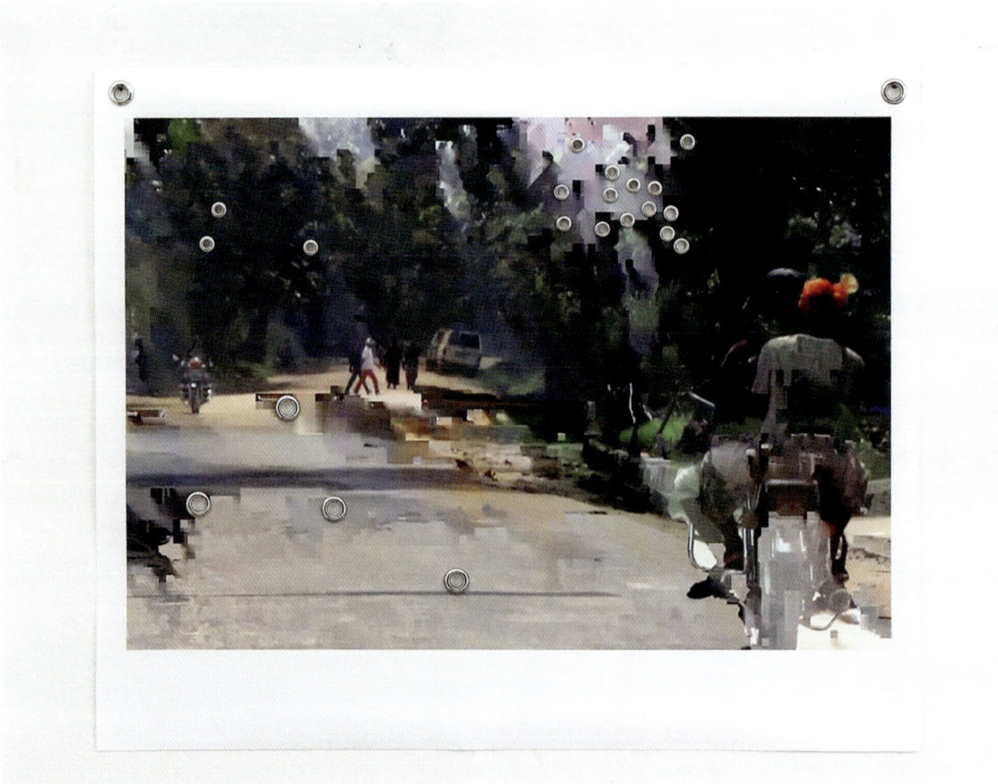

Sandra Mujinga, *Lovely Hosts 1* (2016).
Courtesy of the artist, Croy Nielsen, Vienna and The Approach, London.

homochromia, whereby creatures hide by changing their colour to that of their surroundings. In the video, the image travelling across the screen became fluid, its contours blurred, shifting in and out of focus in a manner similar to the figure behind the covering in *Camouflage Waves 1—3*, though now with colour and contrast as additional layers of confusion.

A less intentional form of obscuration could be found in Mujinga's work, *Lovely Hosts 1—7* (2016), initially shown at Mavra in Berlin. A computer virus disrupted digital photos the artist had taken while travelling across the city of Kisangani in the DRC. It was a glitch, causing pixelations that distorted the images and which the finished photoprint underscored with its perforations and eyelets, as though the paper had been peppered with multiple shots. In *Glitch Feminism: A Manifesto*, Legacy Russell celebrates the glitch as 'a vehicle of refusal, a strategy of non-performance'. By celebrating the mechanical error, even enhancing it, Mujinga harnessed the power of the glitch to open up new vistas of potential meaning in a partial landscape between the physical and the digital.

Stretched Delays 1—4 (2017), a work first shown at Kristiansand Kunsthall, was also included in the Bergen Kunsthall exhibition. Placed on the floor, the work consisted of four crustaceous creatures with curving silicone-covered metal rods for legs and Plexiglas bodies, jealously guarding and blocking the view of LED screens below. The semi-transparent bodies had images printed them, reproducing stills from the screens beneath, making the performers exist in between. From a distance, the various shades of green and brown made it look like it had been dragged along the seabed. This interest in creating works resembling deep-sea creatures has been present

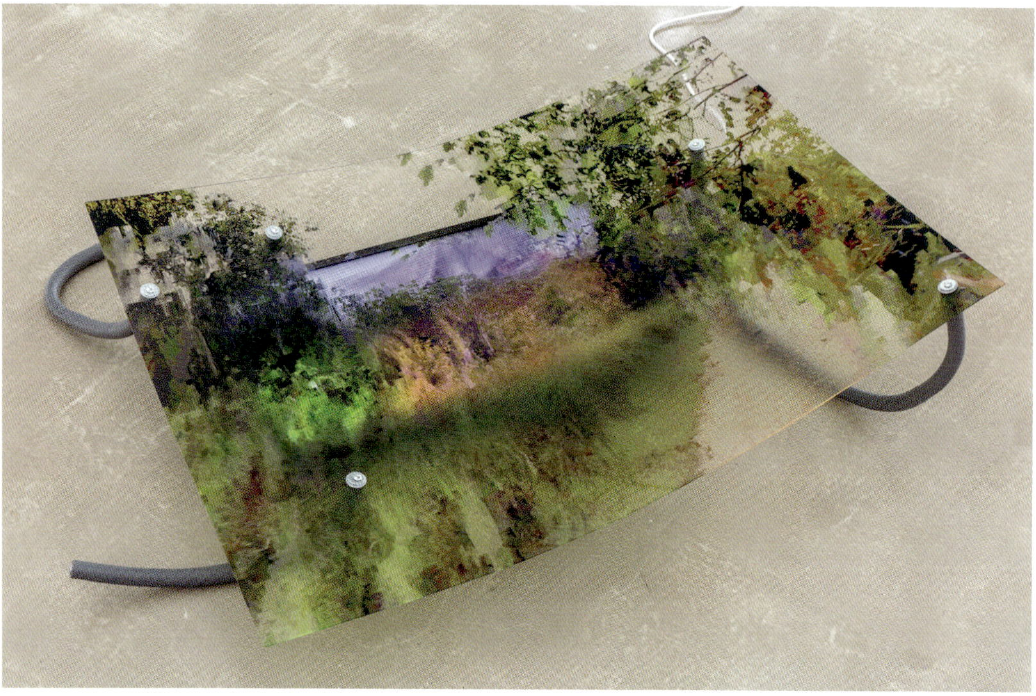

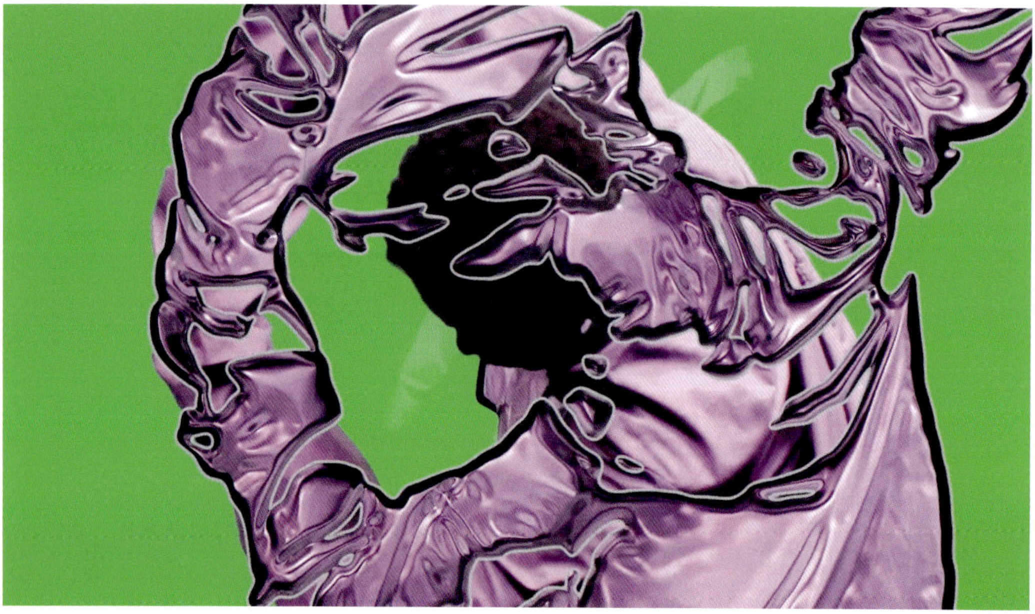

Sandra Mujinga, *Stretched Delays 2,1* (2017). Photo by Tor Simen Ulstein.
Courtesy of the artist, Croy Nielsen, Vienna and The Approach, London.

pp. 20—21 Sandra Mujinga, *Shawl (Elephant Ears)#3,* UNIFORM (2017).
Installation view from *Hoarse Globules* at UKS, Oslo. Photo by Jan Khür. Courtesy of the artist.

in Mujinga's practice from its inception, predating the recent documentary film *My Octopus Teacher* (2020) that has given this particular creature a larger pop-cultural following. In fact, the popularity of the octopus has a longer art-historical trajectory—from Hokusai's 19th-century woodcuts to Jean Painlevé's early and mid-20th-century films dedicated to cephalopods. In 2015, Mujinga created *Scales. Pros and Cons. On Becoming a Sea Creature*, which followed a mermaid-like figure underwater, blurred and blended with digital blobs, a mobile version of the static globules in *Camouflage Waves*. The octopus emerged as a sculptural form in the artist's work at around the same time with *Octo Hoodie/Backpack* (2015), a shape that was adapted in *Octo Handbag* (2017) and in *Octo Clutch/Temporary Home* (2018).

It is not only the creatures of the sea that figure in Mujinga's work, but also animals such as gorillas and elephants. In her solo exhibition, *Real Friends*, at Oslo Kunstforening in 2016, Mujinga included portraits of gorillas, *Humans, on the Other Hand, Lied Easily and Often*. In an on-going body of work from 2016, entitled *Shawl (Elephant Ears)*, Mujinga used her characteristic mix of PVC, acrylic paint and glycerine to create textured sculptures reminiscent of the mammals' large ears. With one side grotesquely flesh-like, it looked like the body part had been amputated, perhaps referencing the widespread poaching of elephants, where the removal of their tusks leaves a gaping, reddish-pink flesh wound on the otherwise grey-brown, thick-skinned animal. This evident empathy with animals in Mujinga's work reminds me of Donna Haraway's notion of 'companion species', from her 2003 manifesto, referring to a genuine love and respect for other creatures on their own terms that does not require anthropomorphism.

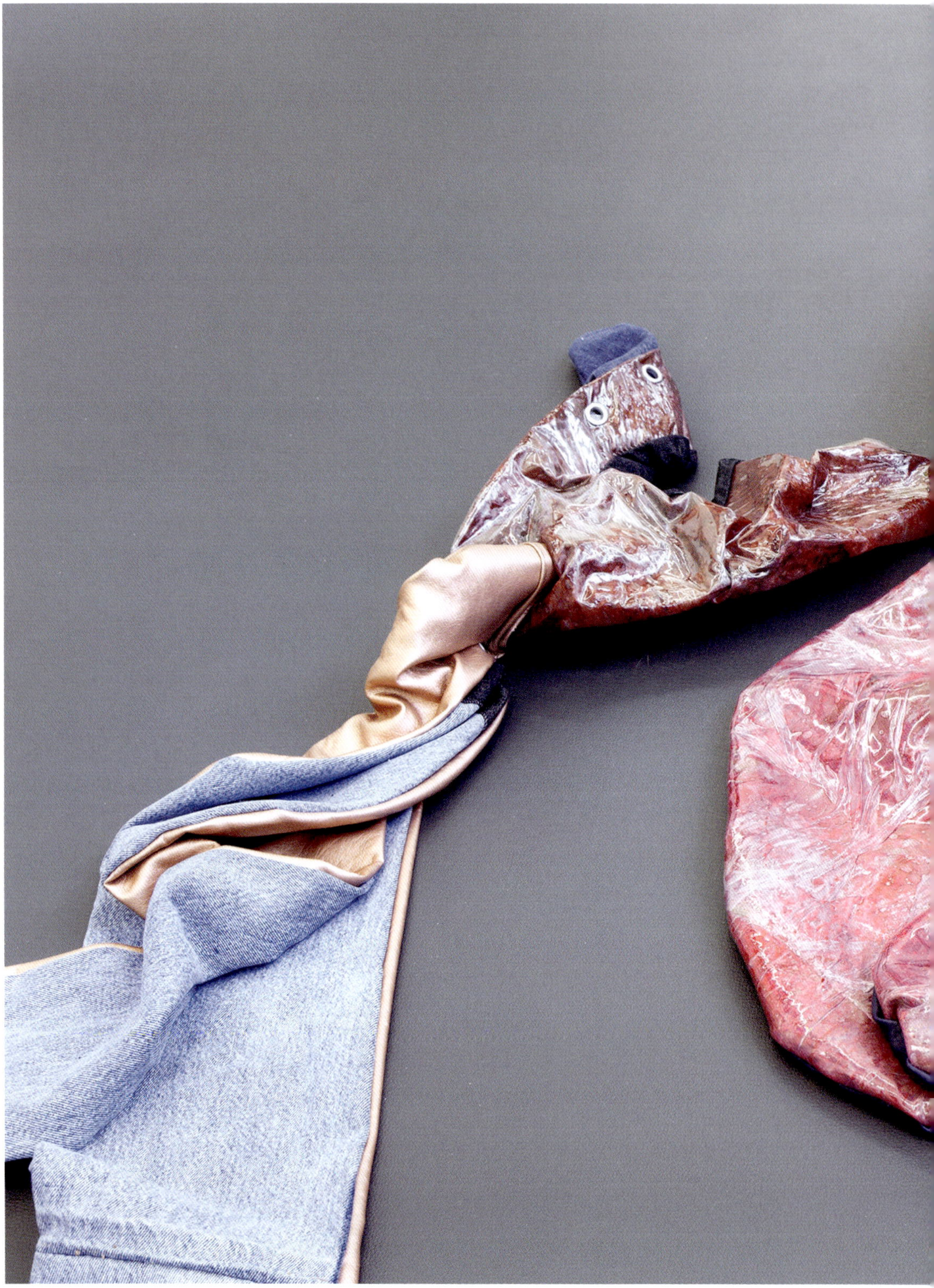

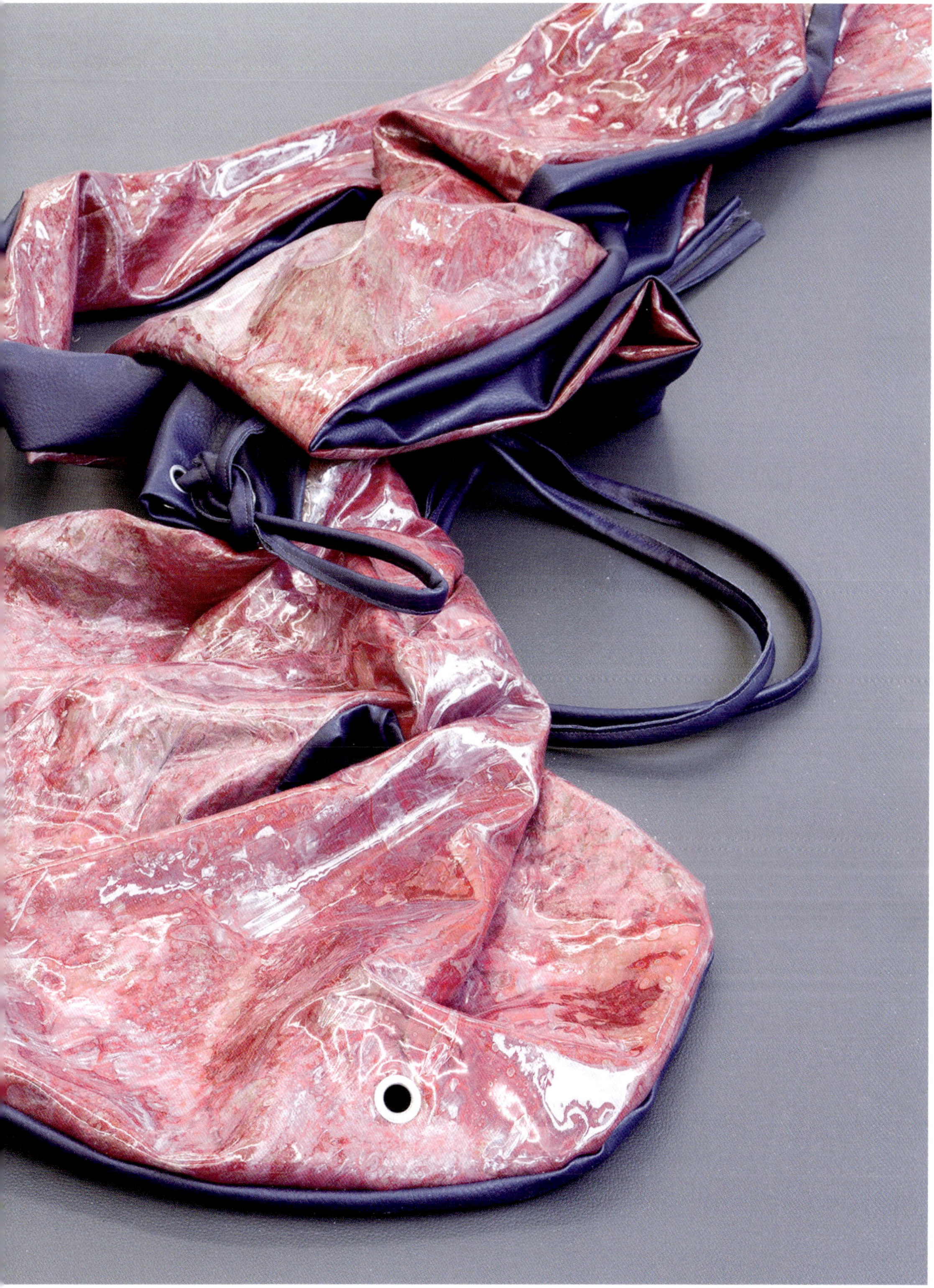

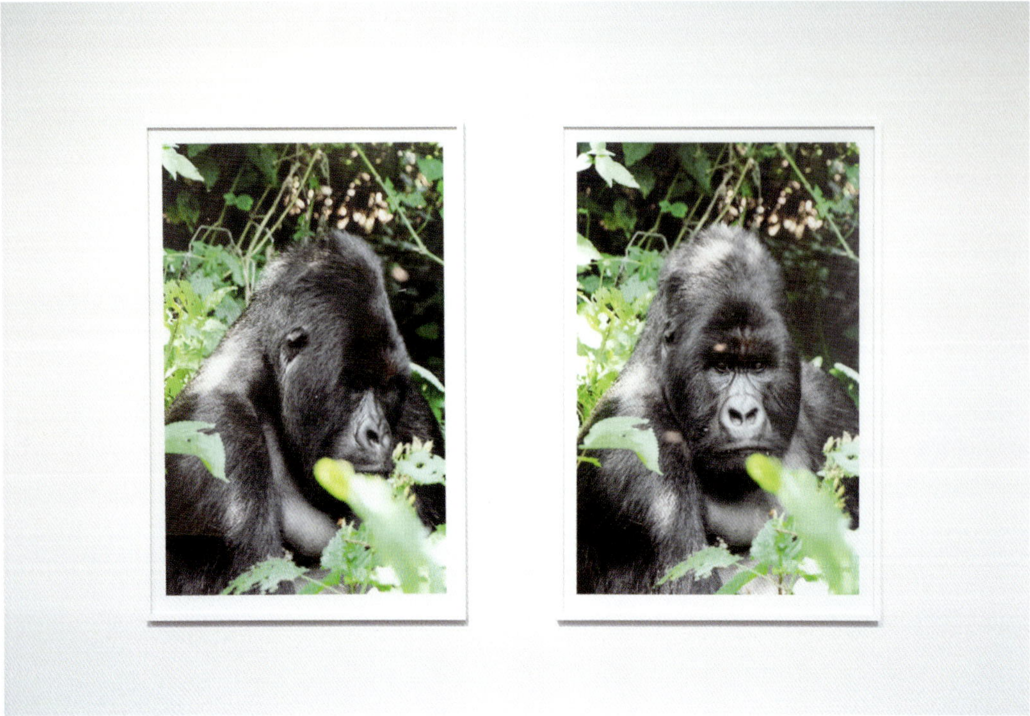

Sandra Mujinga, *Humans, On The Other Hand, Lied Easily and Often 1* (2016).
Photo by Ink Agop. Courtesy of the artist, Croy Nielsen, Vienna, and The Approach, London.

pp. 24—25 Sandra Mujinga, *Ghosting* (2019). Installation view from *Witch Hunt* at Kunsthal Charlottenborg, Copenhagen. Photo by Jan Søndergaard.
Museum of Modern Art in Warsaw.

However, Mujinga goes further with her speculations, and her thinking is more in line with science fiction writers such as Octavia E. Butler from the first lines of whose book, *Dawn*, the gorilla portraits mentioned above derive their title. In a somewhat dystopian post-human vein, Mujinga stated in an interview with *Contemporary And (C&)*, 'Quite often science fiction is about how we will survive, but Butler is not afraid to say that maybe it's not our turn anymore'.

The separation, not only between humans and animals but also between the living and non-living, organic and artificial, gets blurred in Mujinga's use of materials. In the performative work *Atrophic Giants* for the Roskilde Music Festival in 2018, the artist's 'elephant ears' expanded into the silhouette of a whole elephant, mutated to erase the distinction between the epidermal layers by burning acrylic and combining PVC, glycerine and oil paint, resulting in the large flakes of plasticky, singed skin. The same technique was used to create an even larger work, *Ghosting* (2019), installed like a garish tarpaulin across the exhibition space at Kistefos Sculpture Park in Jevnaker, north-west of Oslo, for the group show *TEMPO TEMPO TEMPO*, curated by Rhea Dall in 2019. This work also incorporated denim, another material Mujinga has used repeatedly, often in combination with other textiles, for instance, in her contribution to the Norwegian Sculpture Biennial, *Clear as Day* (2017). The title was playfully negated in the performance where models used Mujinga's oversized, 'wearable sculptures' with large hoods to prevent any clear view of their bodies.

Mujinga's titles often contain layers of meaning that are sometimes contradictory. *Ghosting* refers both to the strange presence of this piece of partially

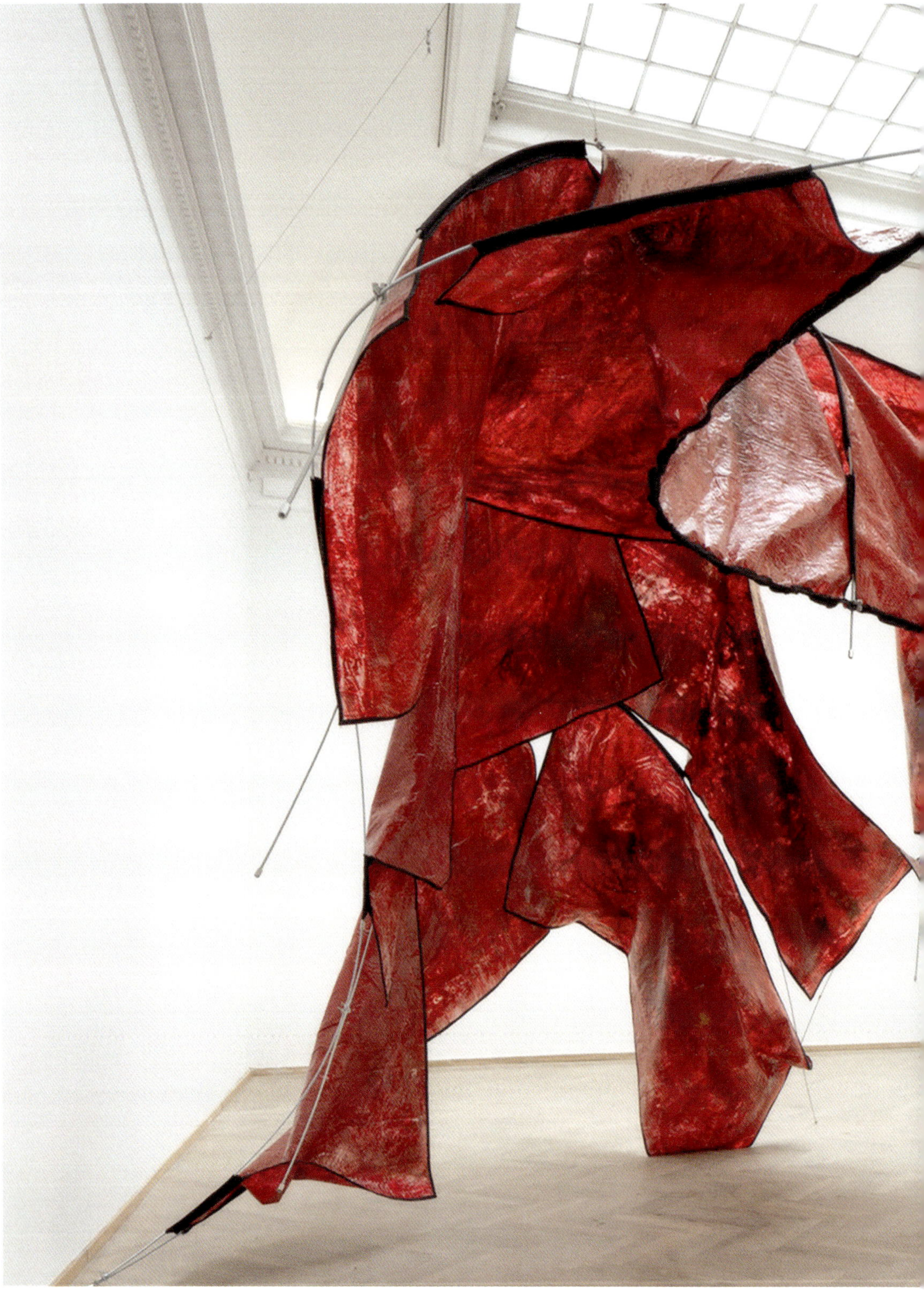

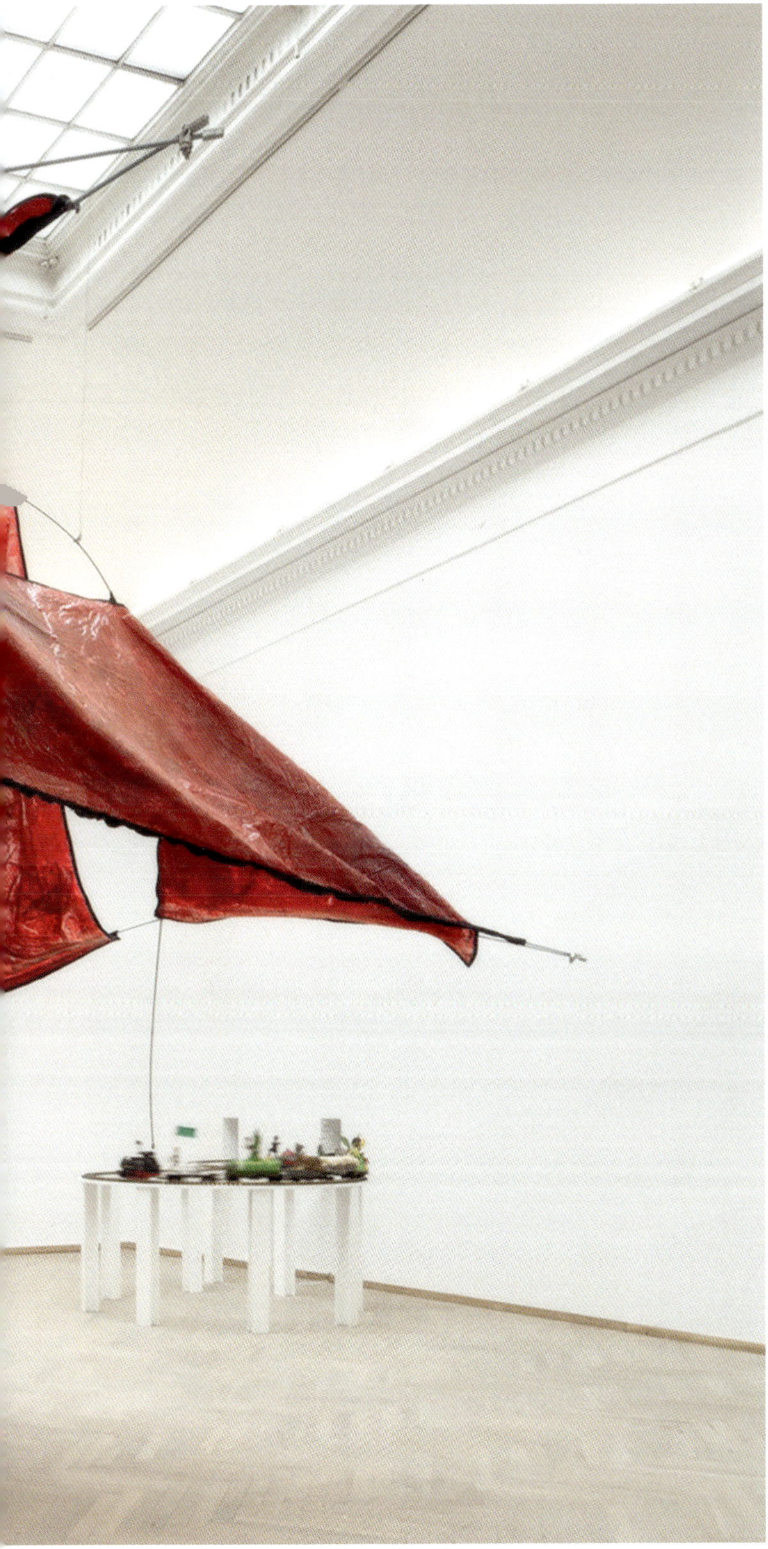

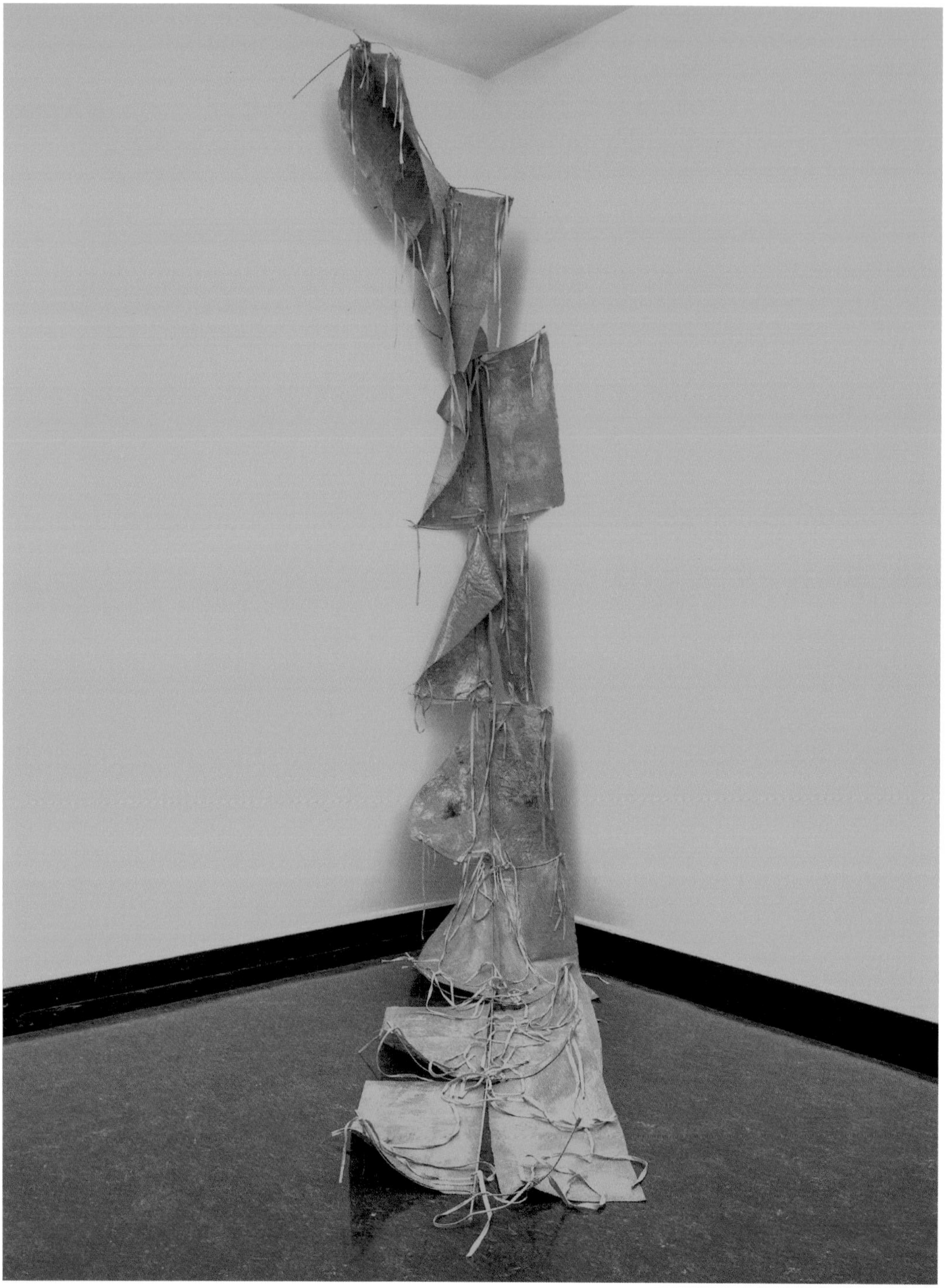

Sandra Mujinga, *Coiling* (2019), Installation view from *SONW—Shadow of New Worlds* at Bergen Kunsthall. Photo by Thor Brødreskift.

melded, burnt, damaged material and to the largely online phenomenon of ghosting, where one simply stops responding to a conversation partner, disappearing like a ghost. By using acronyms for many of her titles, Mujinga also plays with the penchant for minimising characters or the use of absurd hashtags, doomed to fail as one-offs in the prevailing argot of digital culture. Her longest to date is *YISIFOTMATABOJTMIDTIPFMBRPMFWWC* (2016), which stands for: 'Yesterday I stood in front of the mirror and told a bunch of jokes to myself, I don't think I performed for myself, but rather prepared myself for what would come'. A snappier acronym was *SONW—Shadow of New Worlds*, the title used for the exhibition at Bergen Kunsthall and its accompanying catalogue.

Up until the spring of 2019, my only encounter with Sandra Mujinga was through her exhibited or performed work. Concomitantly with the opening at Kistefos, Mujinga was awarded the first solo exhibition in new series *SOLO OSLO*, which I had conceived when I took up a permanent position at the Munch Museum. As a curator, one's relationship with an artist tends to change once they become a future exhibitor. One moves from the outside—as an engaged viewer or fervent admirer—to the inside. One gains a better understanding of the artist's process, the fine details of the work's becoming. One loses the approximation of an objective view, a blissfully unaware delight in the finished work. Subsequently, I viewed every new exhibition of Mujinga's work with new eyes, focusing on the specifics, doing a mental search for how this work related to earlier ones I had seen or the one the artist was making for the exhibition at MUNCH, as the museum had by now become known.

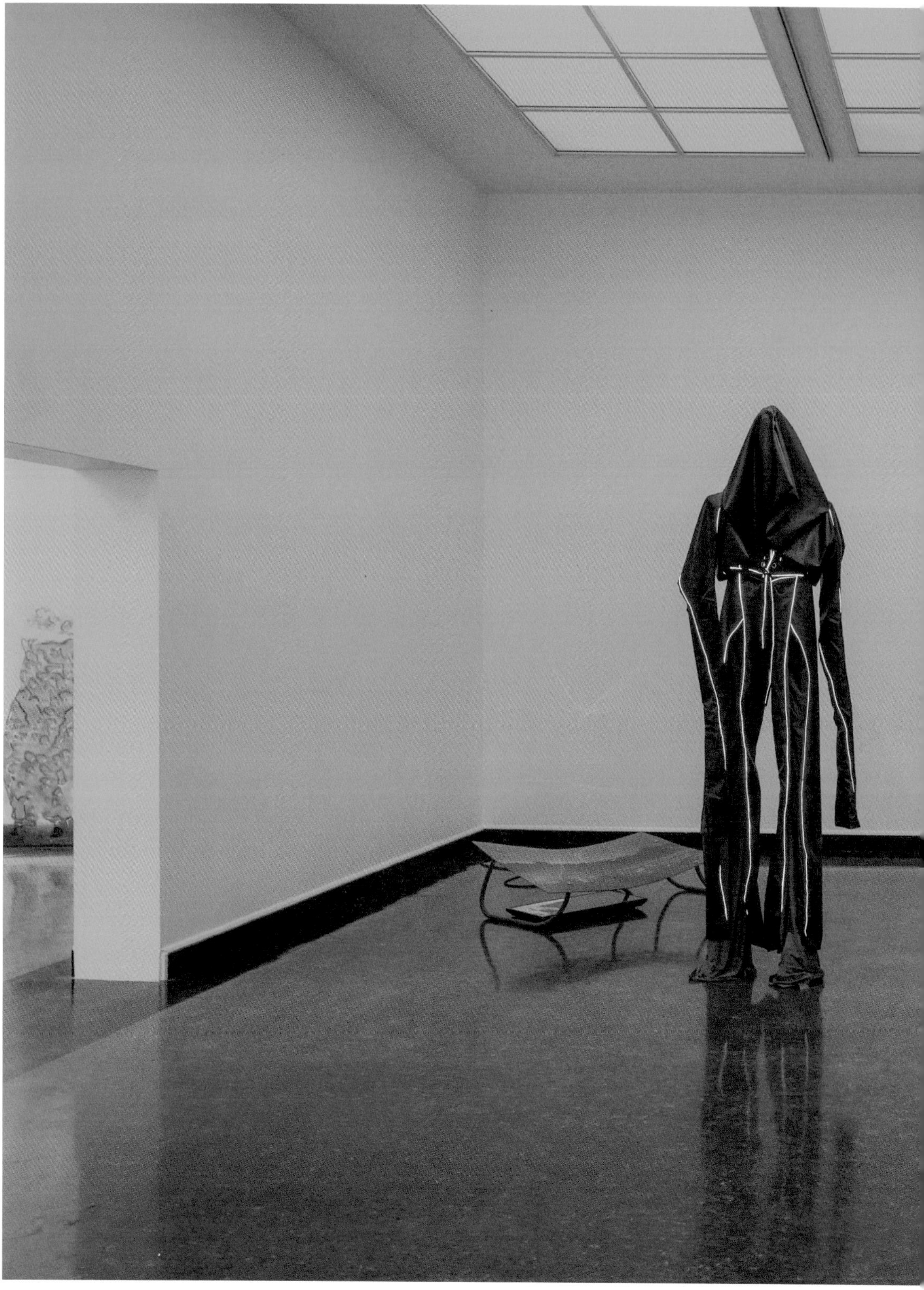

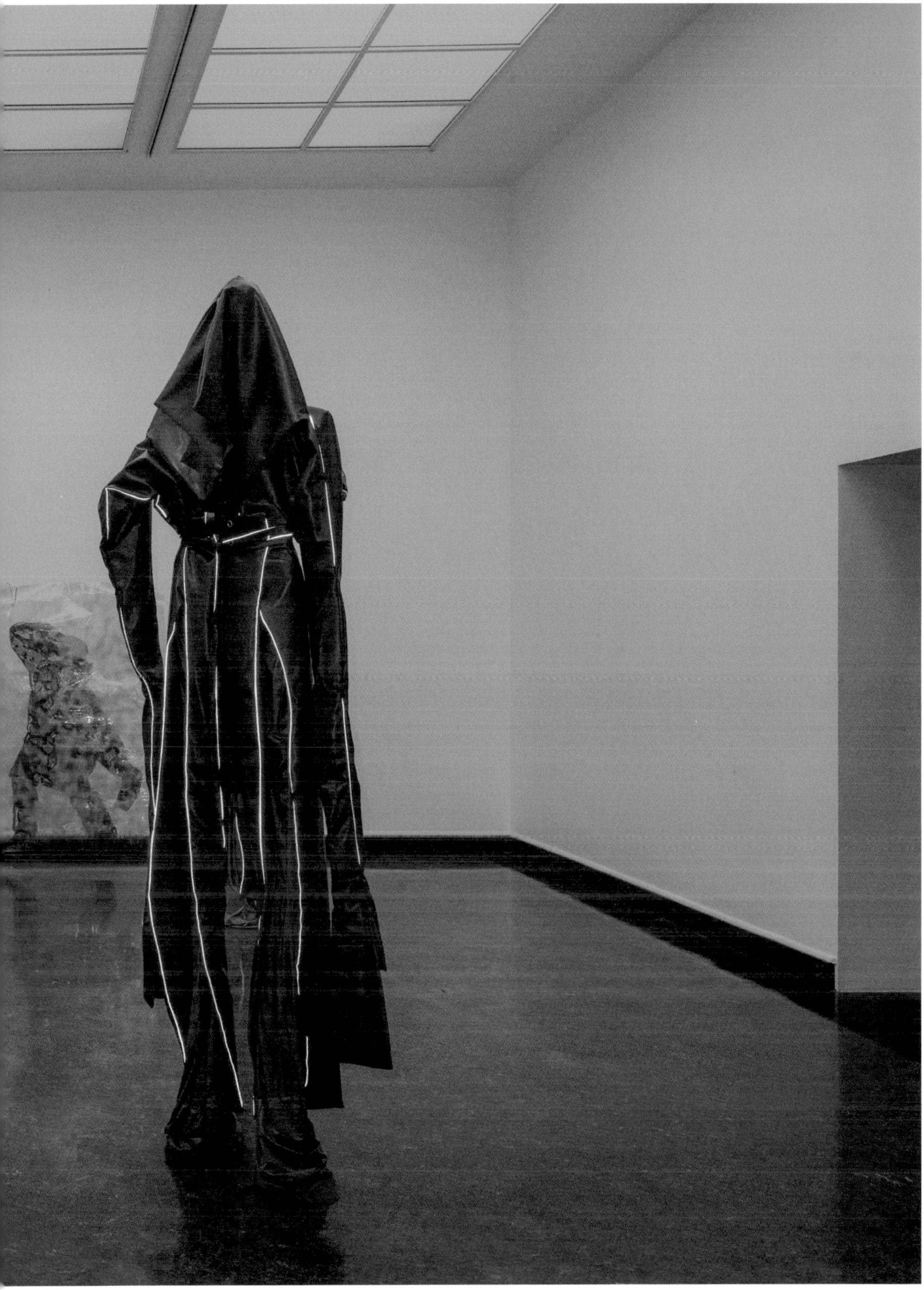

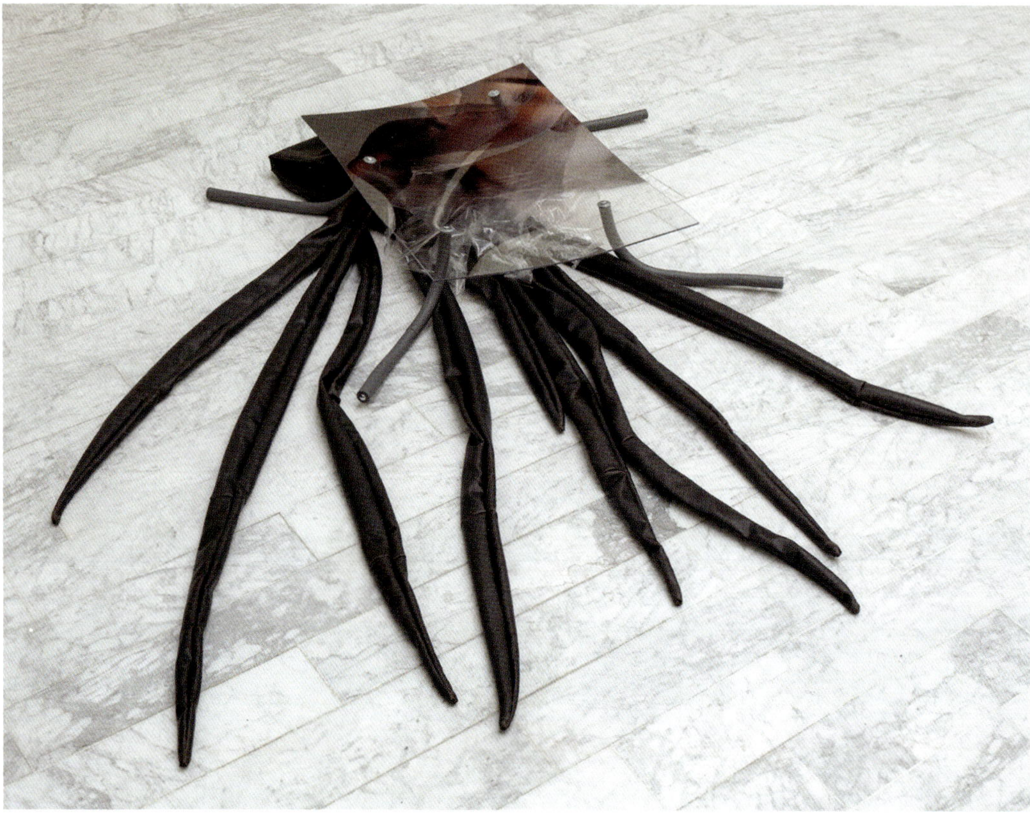

Sandra Mujinga, *Octo Clutch/Temporary Home* (2018).
Photo by Jan Søndergaard. Courtesy the artist and The Approach, London.

pp. 28—29 Sandra Mujinga, *SONW—Shadow of New Worlds.*
Installation view from Bergen Kunsthall, Bergen. Photo by Thor Brødreskift.

The *SOLO OSLO* show was initially scheduled for October 2020, then it was delayed for over a year-and-a-half due to the pandemic and the postponement of the opening of the new MUNCH museum building. Mujinga's exhibition finally went on display in January 2022.

Since our collaboration started in 2019, Mujinga's career as an emerging artist has 'taken off' as the artspeak-prone actors from *You Are All You Need* might have put it. Mujinga's first solo exhibition at her gallery Croy Nielsen in Vienna, *Seasonal Pulses*, in spring 2019 introduced the hooded, long-legged, flared-trousered figures of *Mókó, Libwá, Zómi* and *Nhámá*, 'named for the order in which they will exist in the future' (their names translate from Lingala as 1, 9, 10 and 100, respectively). These were also included in the exhibition at Bergen Kunsthall, which opened at the end of 2019 and closed just before the pandemic restricted freedom of movement at the start of 2020. The transportation of works was less impeded, however, and *Mókó, Libwá, Zómi* and *Nhámá* travelled together with *Flo* and *Coiling* to Vleeshal in Middelburg in the Netherlands as part of a different, smaller version of the exhibition in Bergen in late 2020, before moving on to the Gothenburg Museum of Art in summer 2021. At the same time, the *Nokturnal Kinship* figures travelled to the MOMENTA Biennale in Montreal, together with *Disruptive Pattern; Ghosting* travelled to a group show at the Kunsthal Charlottenborg in Copenhagen; and *Octo Clutch/Temporary Home* made an appearance at Nottingham Contemporary in the UK. Mujinga's practice encompasses far more than I could hope to address in this one text, and many of her other works also made their way across land and sea to reach other audiences.

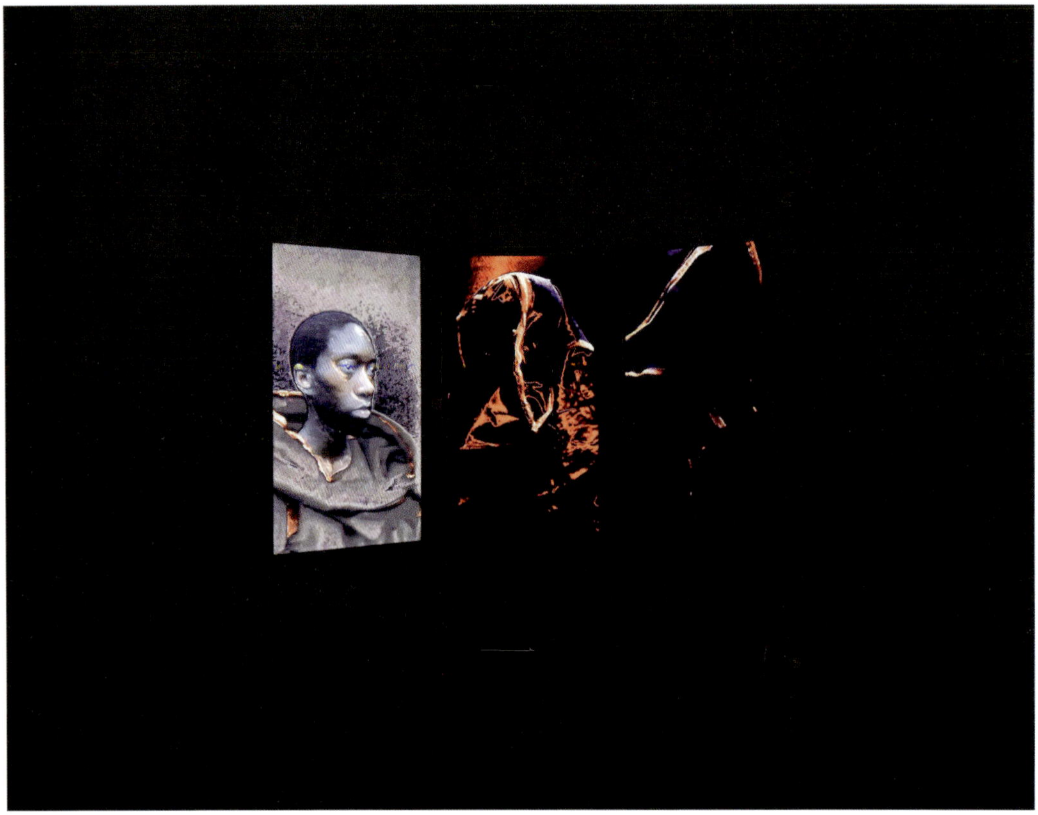

Sandra Mujinga, *Pervasive Light* (2021). Installation view from *2021 Triennial: Soft Water Hard Stone* at the New Museum, New York. Photo by Dario Lasagni. Courtesy of the artist, Croy Nielsen, Vienna and The Approach. London.

pp. 34—35 Sandra Mujinga, installation view from *Preis der Nationalgalerie* at Hamburger Bahnhof, Berlin (2021). Photo by Jens Ziehe. Courtesy of the artist, Croy Nielsen, Vienna and The Approach, London.

Mujinga produced a number of new works during the pandemic, including a series of tall, textile-clad figures for the exhibition *Spectral Keepers* at her London gallery, The Approach. These later travelled to MUSEION in Bolzano, Italy. In May 2021, Mujinga premiered her three-screen work, shaped like windows, for her solo show, *Worldview*, at the Swiss Institute in New York. Just days later, Mujinga was awarded Sandefjord Kunstforening's Art Prize of 200,000 NOK for the video triptych *Pervasive Light* (2021), which was subsequently included in the New Museum Triennial in New York at the end of October 2021. That same month, Mujinga was awarded the prestigious Preis der Nationalgalerie. In her nominee exhibition at the Hamburger Bahnhof in Berlin, Mujinga showed two new works: *Sentinels of Change* (2021) and *Reworlding Remains* (2021). The former, a floor-based installation, included the remains of some imagined prehistoric creature, watched over by a tall figure, draped in overlaid textiles, like basket-weave or crocheted shawls. One of the guards stood over a welded metal-rod construction with tattered fabric hanging from its frame. According to the artist, the weaving of the textile with its frayed ends suggested a skin that could either be growing anew or on the brink of collapse; and the shape, an outline of a dinosaur, acted as 'a speculative site to imagine new bodies', going backwards in time in order to reconceive the future. In the next room, three further sentinels hovered ominously like spectres of death, more bedraggled and disturbing than their figurative relatives in Mujinga's other works, *Spectral Keepers, Nokturnal Kinship* and *Mókó, Libwá, Zómi* and *Nhámá*.

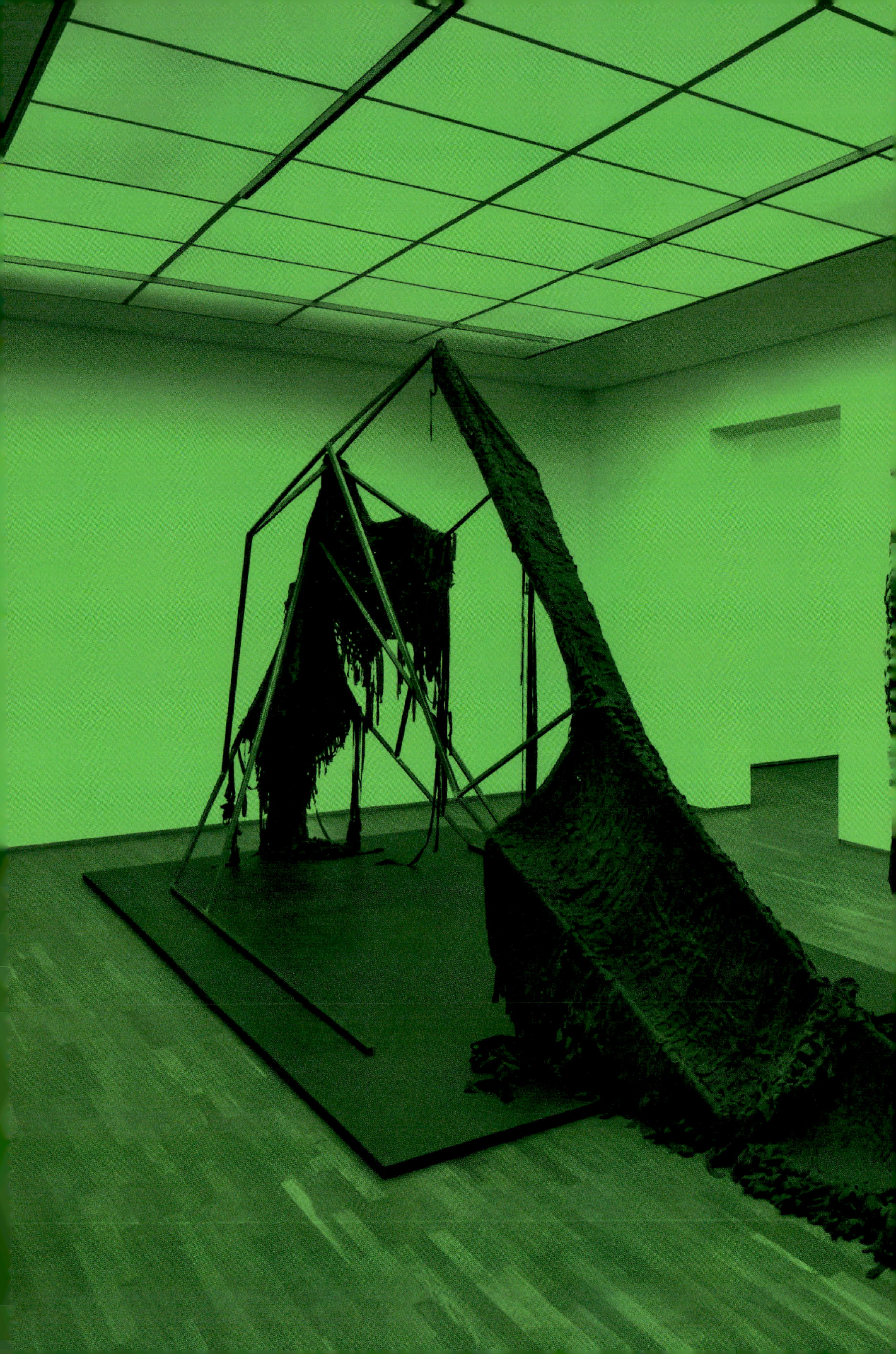

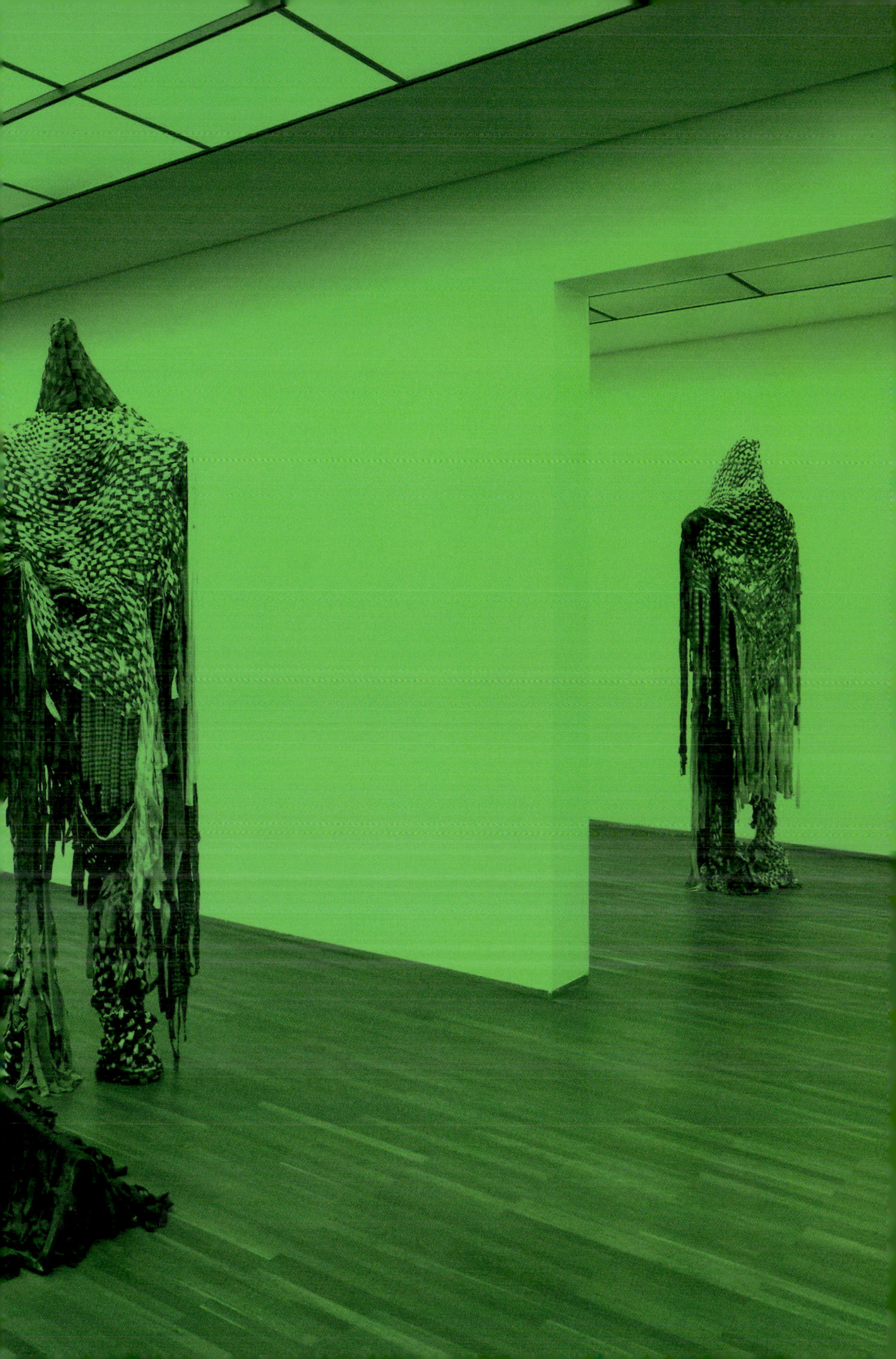

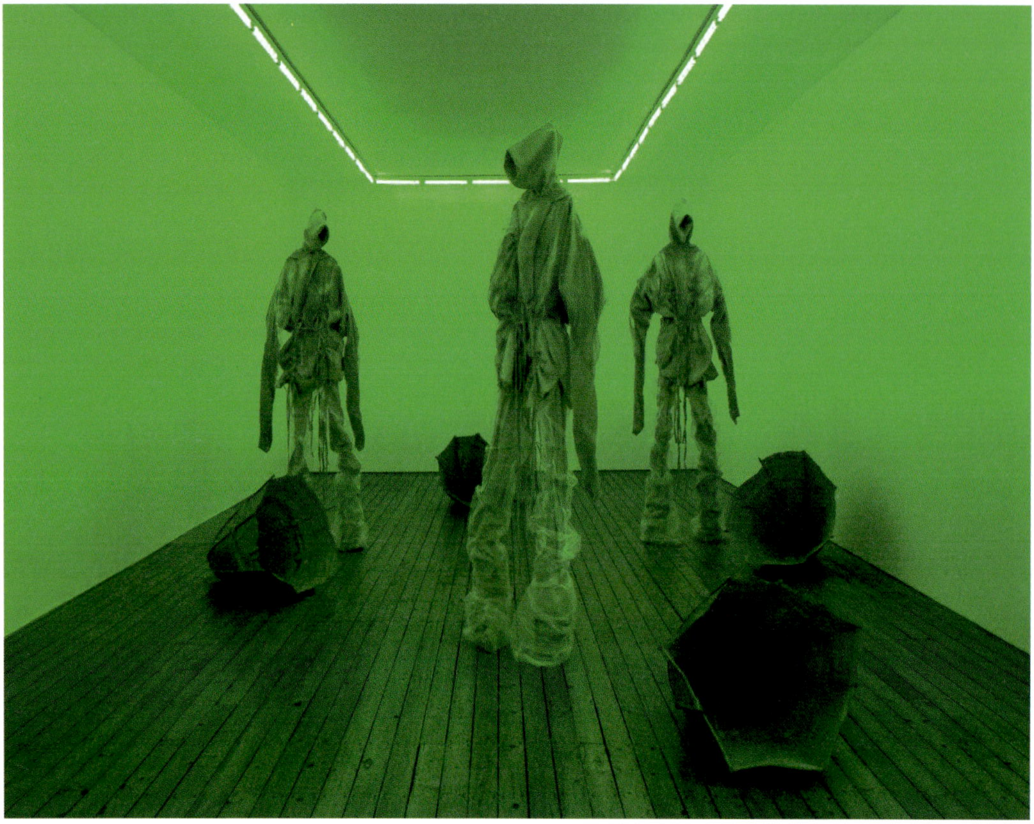

Sandra Mujinga, installation view from *Spectral Keepers* at The Approach, London (2021). Photo by Lewis Ronald. Courtesy of the artist and The Approach, London.

pp. 38—39 Sandra Mujinga, *Worldview* (2021). Installation view from the Swiss Institute, New York. Courtesy of the artist, Croy Nielsen, Vienna and The Approach, London.

In Mujinga's new commission for MUNCH, there were elements that can be traced back to other exhibitions in her oeuvre. The triptych videos from Sandefjord Kunstforening and the New Museum Triennial had expanded into a larger, three-dimensional trio of Plexiglas cubicles. The material harked back to the semi-transparent Plexiglas of earlier works such as *Camouflage Waves 1—3* and *Stretched Delays 1—4*. In the vast space on level 10 of MUNCH, however, the opaque planes served as projection surfaces that refracted and blurred the animated figure. The result of a collaboration with designer, Saphira Nancy, Mujinga's new figure had antecedents in *Flo*, in its strange muscularity, but also in the 'deep sea' works with the mermaid and octopus. The animated sequences were projected from the mouths of three monster-like figures, their metal scales offering a departure from Mujinga's usual penchant for textiles and glycerine/PVC compounds as approximations of skin. Nonetheless, the anthropomorphism of both the monsters and the animated figure remained, though they departed even further from any concrete resemblance to humans. Describing them as 'an alien invasion of the office', Mujinga created hybrid creatures that might equally belong on the seabed or in the realm of the extra-terrestrial. The artist's characteristic use of green light figured again in this exhibition, erasing the contours of the space as it met the darkened floor and walls. The artificial corridor Mujinga added to the gallery on level 10 at MUNCH resembled the one she created for her exhibition *Worldview*, where she reconfigured the basement space at the Swiss Institute. The extra hallway at MUNCH, however, had the addition of one-way glass, which played with the relationship between 'who gets to look at whom' as visitors enter the installation. The gentle soundtrack of synth and strings, resembling

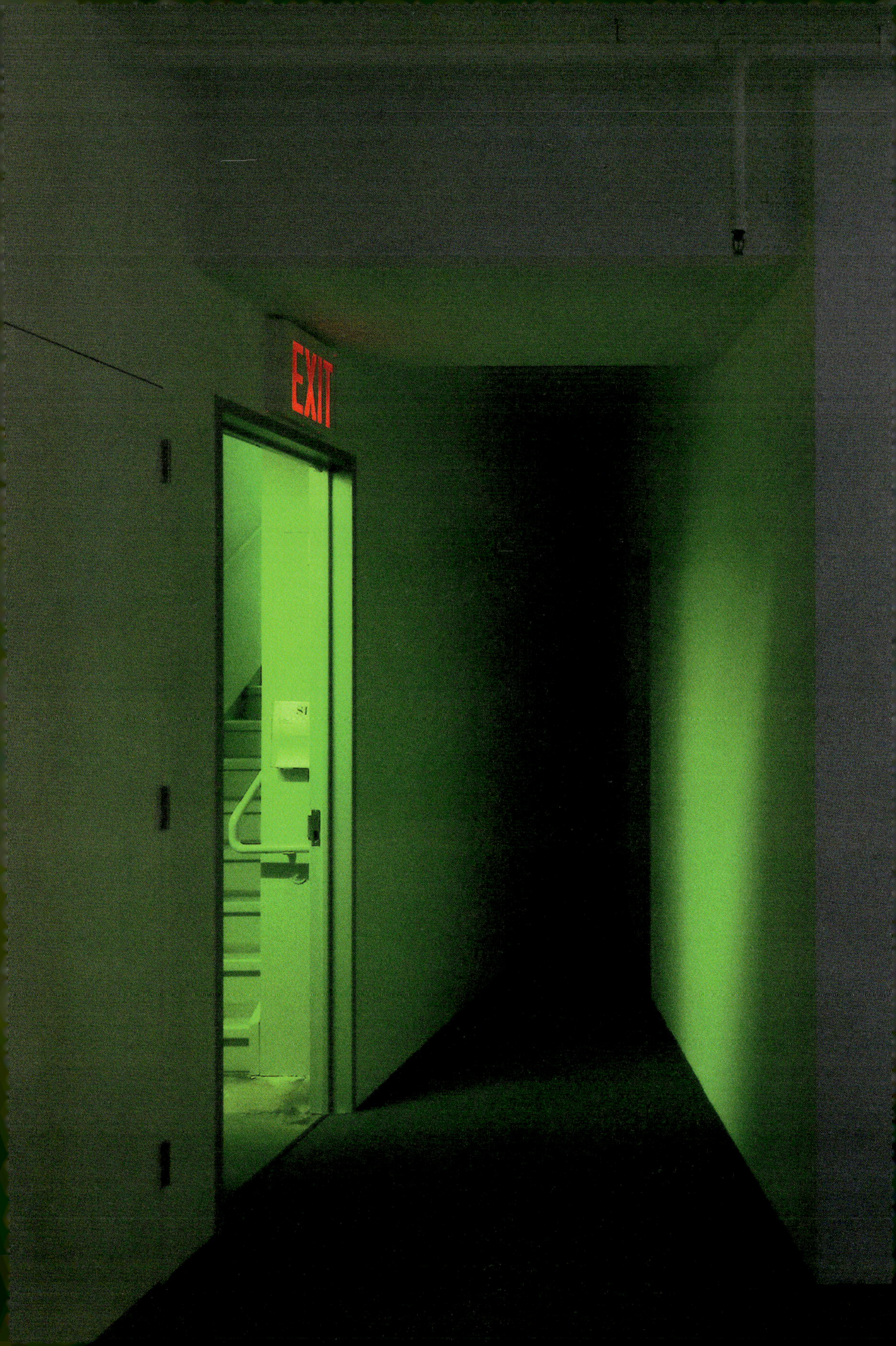
EXIT

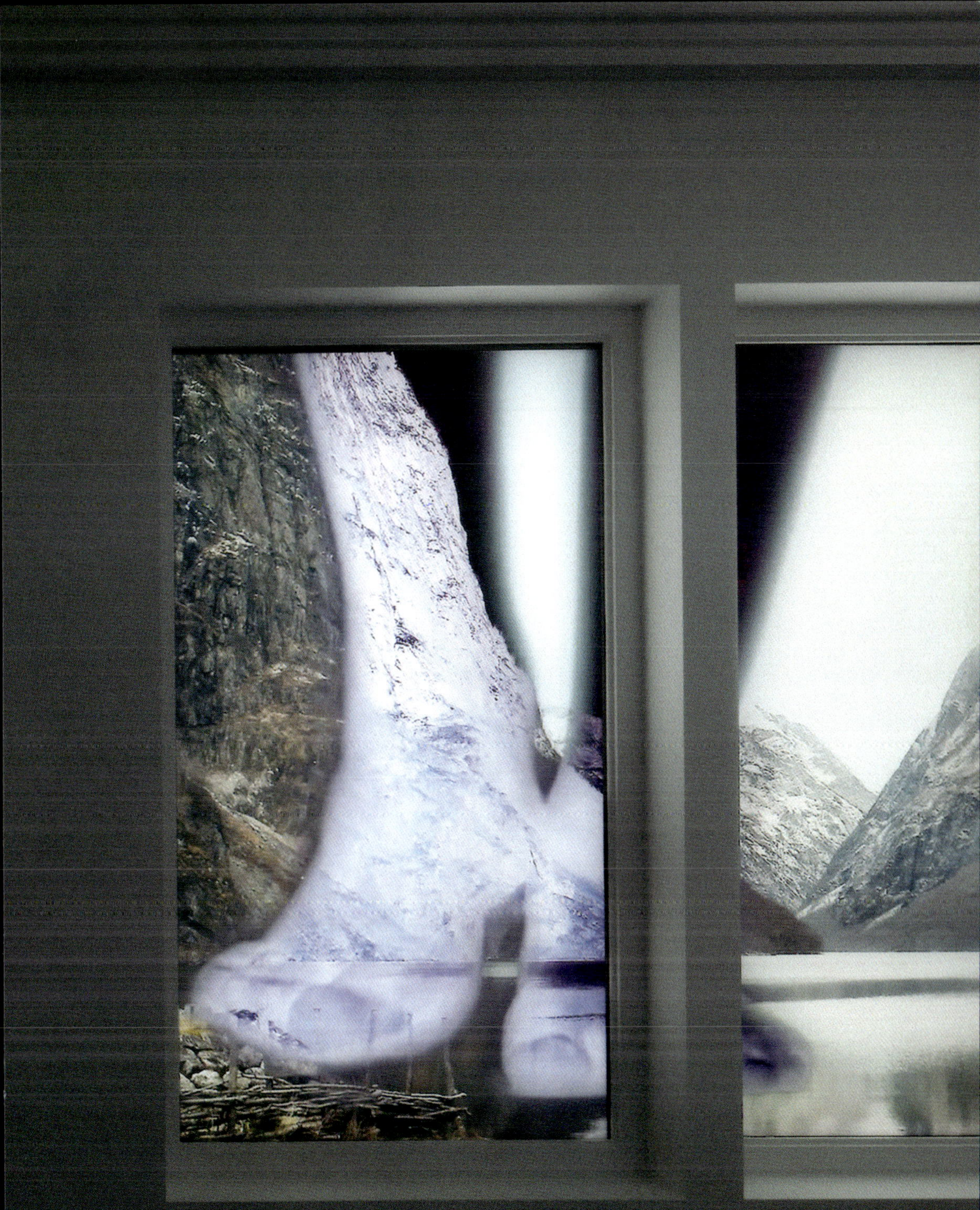

that of *Flo*, added a subtle auditory dimension to this new installation. Where did the creature come from? What had it seen that made it run? What tales from beyond the abyss might it narrate? As Gabi Ngcobo noted in her text for the Berlin Biennale:

> Addressing history in the present is to speak to a future unknown. Belonging to the generation of the current moment, we cannot immediately understand, in relative opacity, how the events of the present will affect our futures.

Like Jemisin's orogene, Sandra Mujinga's work might offer an indication of the impact of the events of past and present on the future. Although disturbing, this power to 'sess', however speculative it might be, should be be treasured as a route to greater insight into the here and now. For every new work, standing on the shoulders of its forebears, Mujinga opens up uncharted vistas of understanding and new routes to reflection.

Cited works (in order of citation)

p.9 N.K. Jemisin, *The Fifth Season* (2015)
p.9 Sandra Mujinga, 'You Are All You Need', in Sandra Mujinga, *SONW—Shadow of New Worlds* (2020)
p.11 *Mad Max: Beyond Thunderdome*, dir. George Miller and George Ogilvie (1985)
p.15 Édouard Glissant, *Poetics of Relation*, trans. Betsy Wing (1997)
p.15 Gabi Ngcobo, 'Dear History, We Don't Need Another Hero', catalogue 10th Berlin Biennale (2016)
p.17 Legacy Russell, *Glitch Feminism: A Manifesto* (2020)
p.19 *My Octopus Teacher* (film), dir. Pippa Ehrlich and James Reed (2020)
p.19 *The Octopus (La Pieuvre)* (film), dir. Jean Painlevé (1927)
p.19 *The Love Life of the Octopus (Les Amours de la Pieuvre)* (film), dir. Jean Painlevé and Geneviève Hamon (1967)
p.19 Donna Haraway, *The Companion Species Manifesto: Dogs, People, and Significant Otherness* (2003)
p.23 Octavia E. Butler, *Dawn* (1987)
p.23 Sheila Feruzi, 'Manoeuvring Through the Dark with Sandra Mujinga', C& (14 January 2020)

SANDRA MUJINGA

CLOSED SPACE, OPEN WORLD

SOLO OSLO
MUNCH—2022

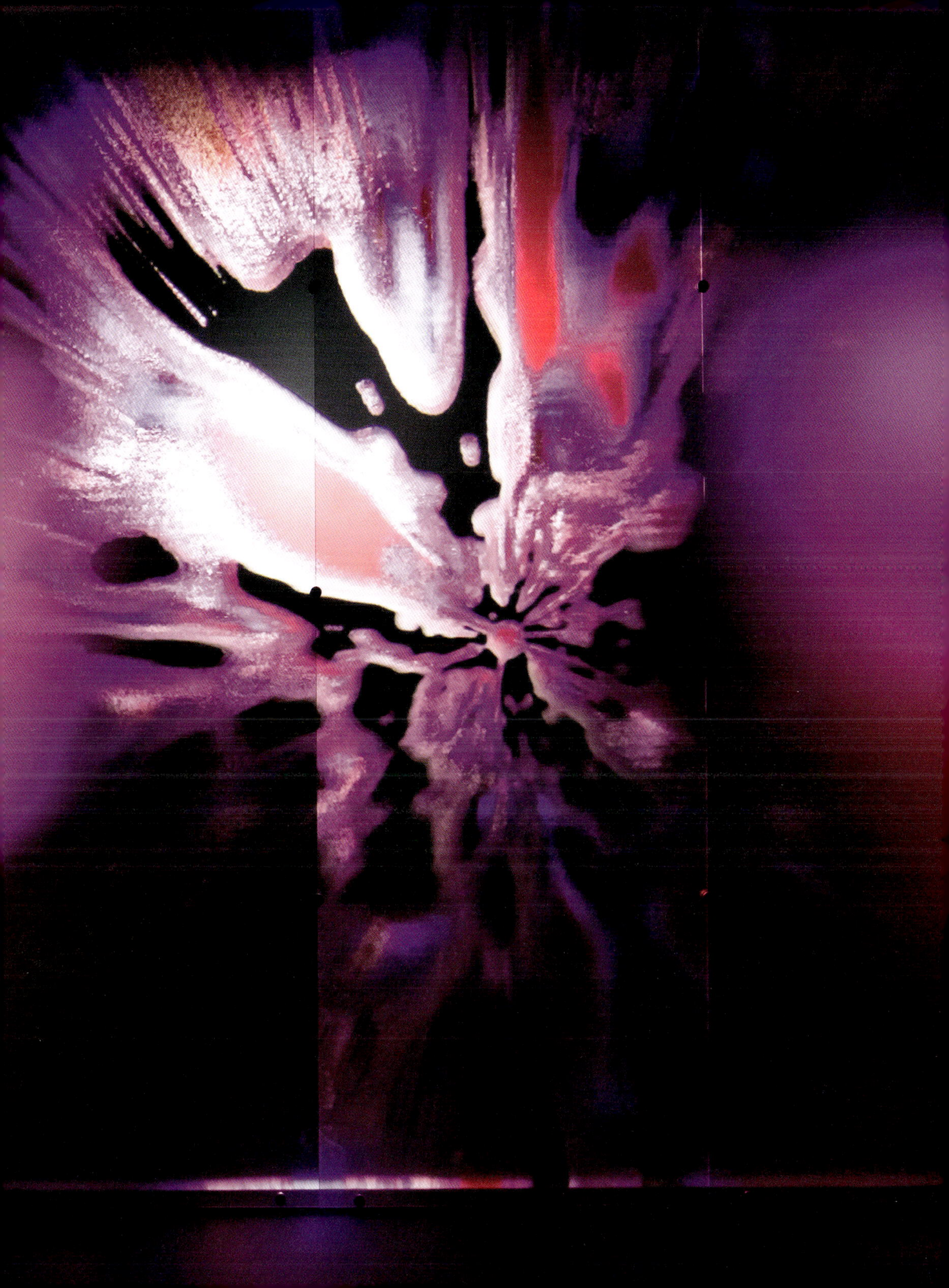

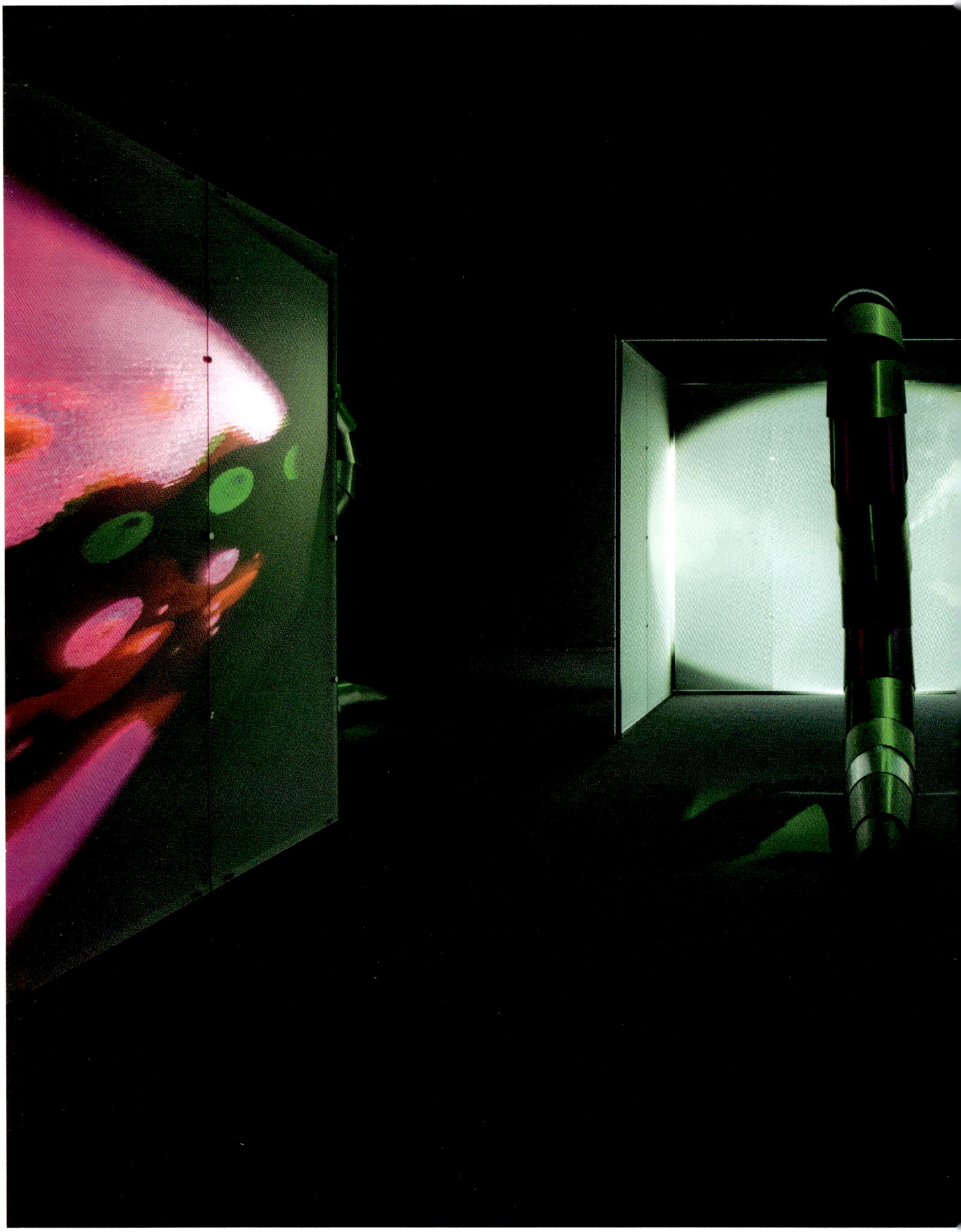

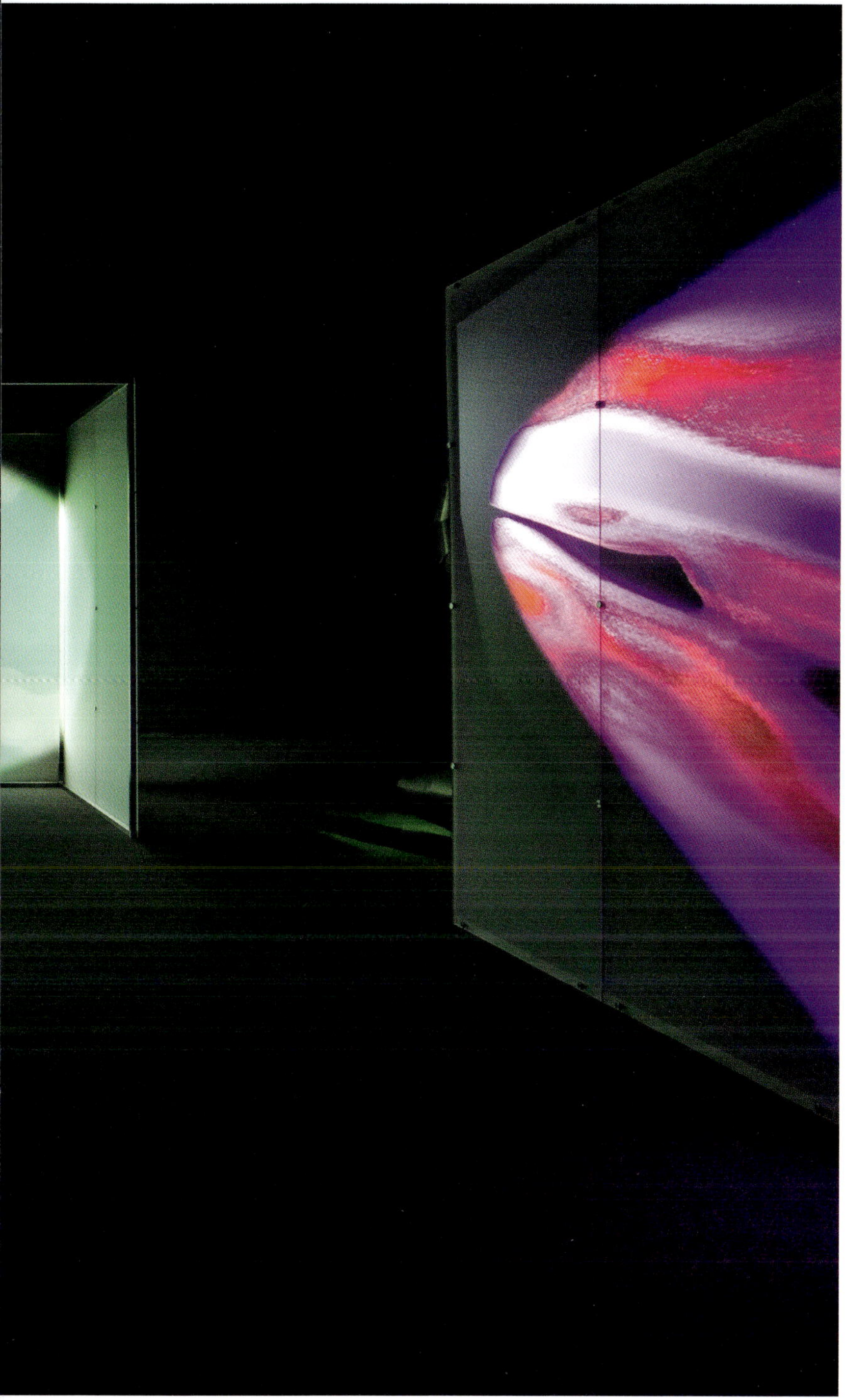

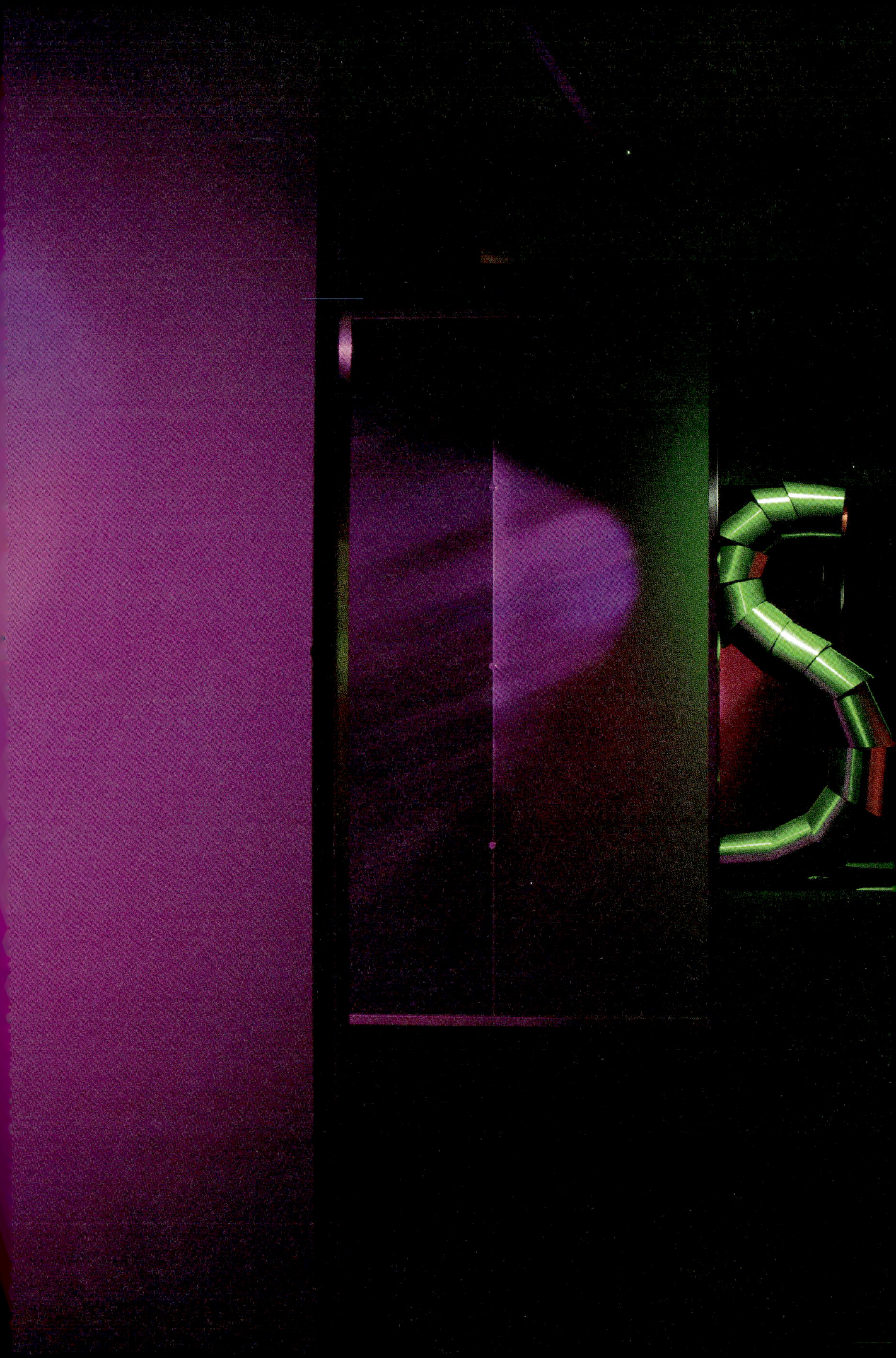

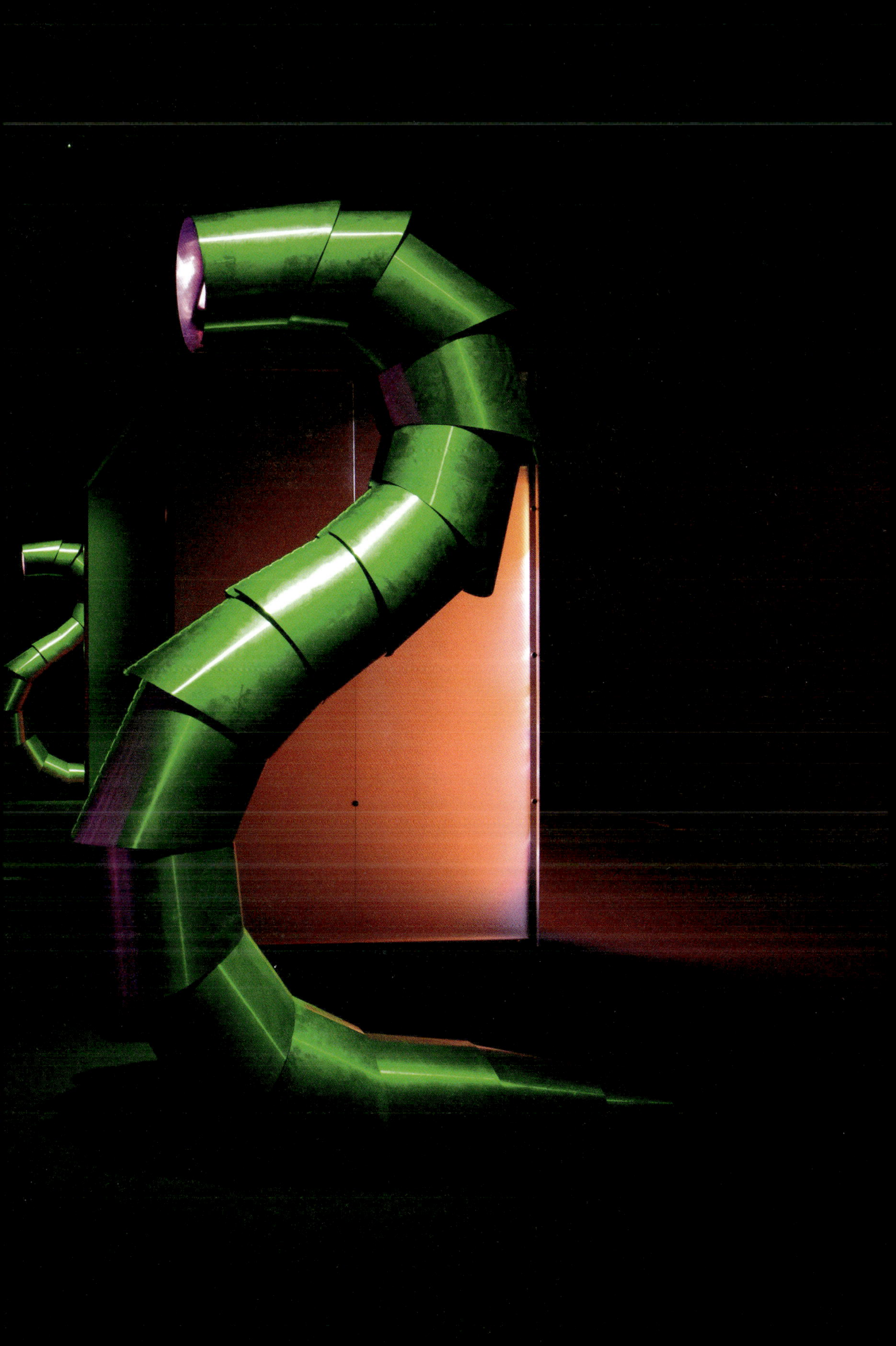

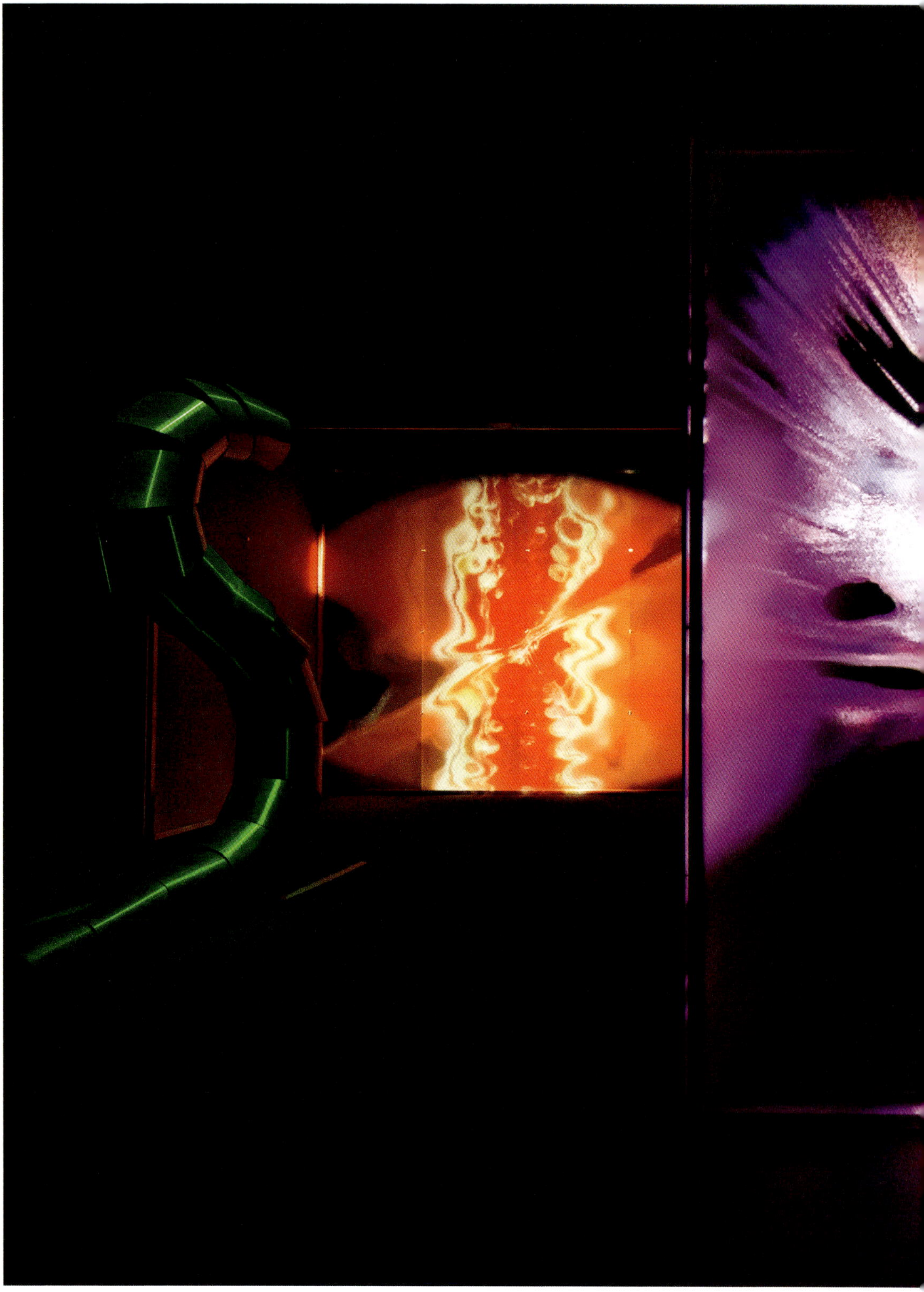

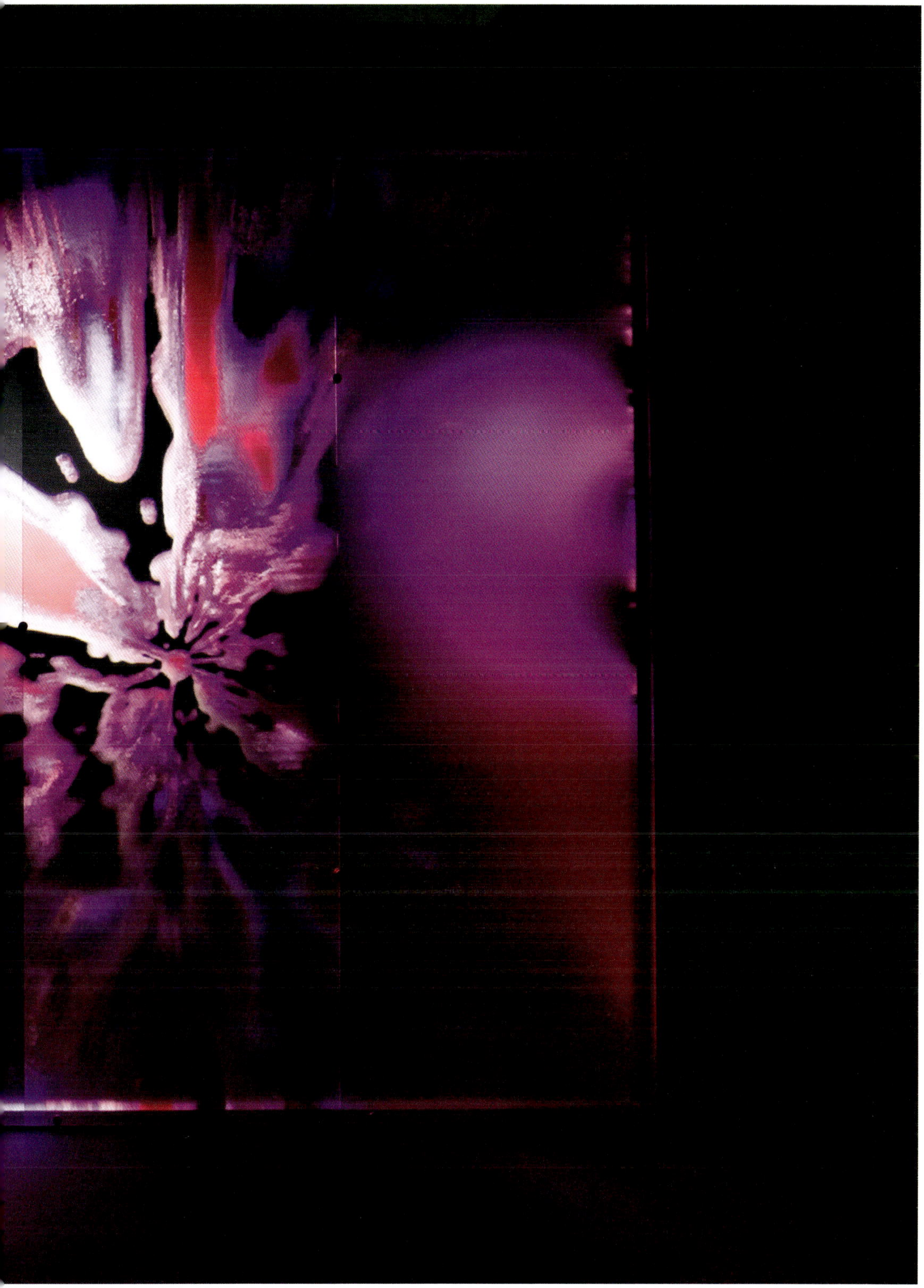

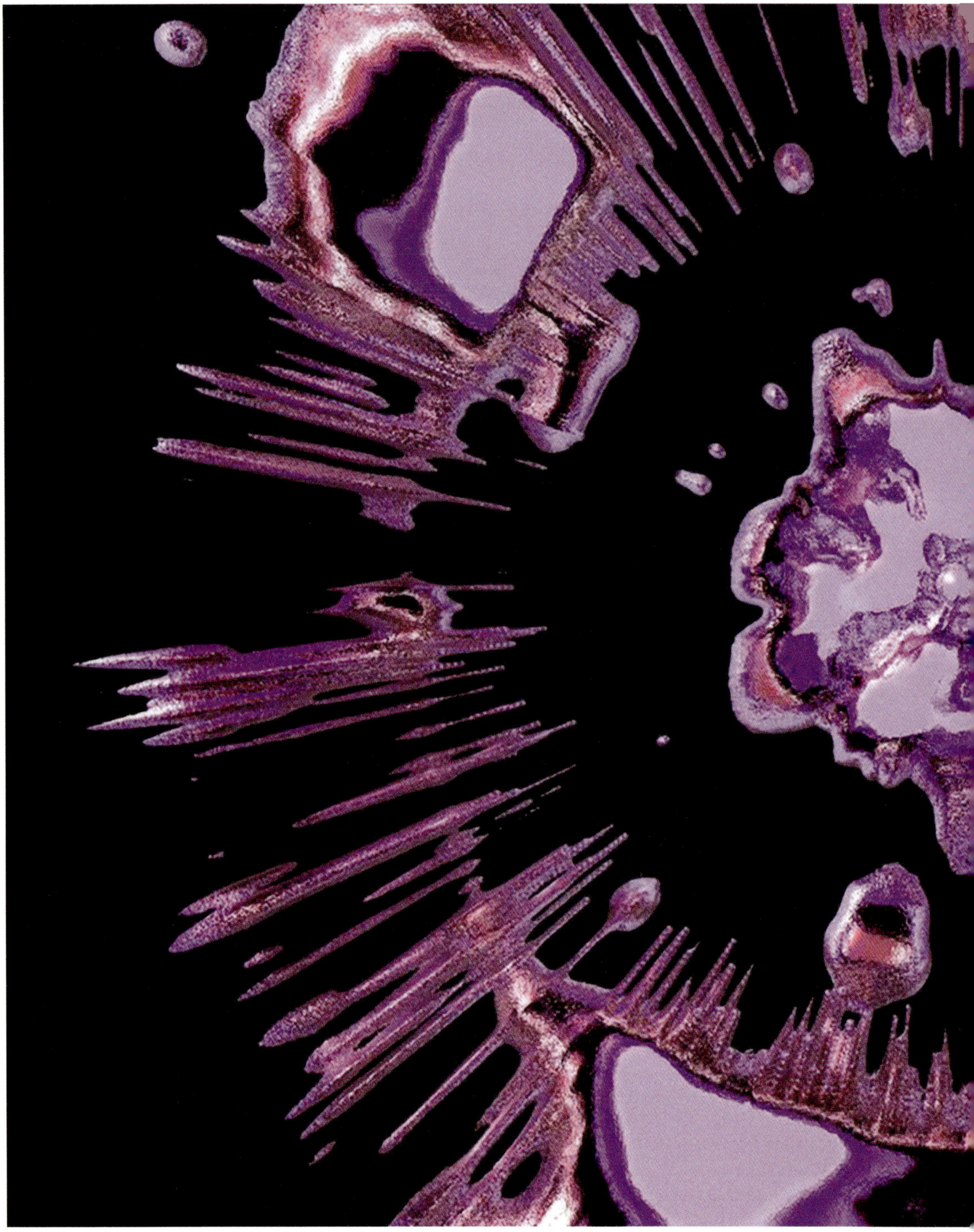

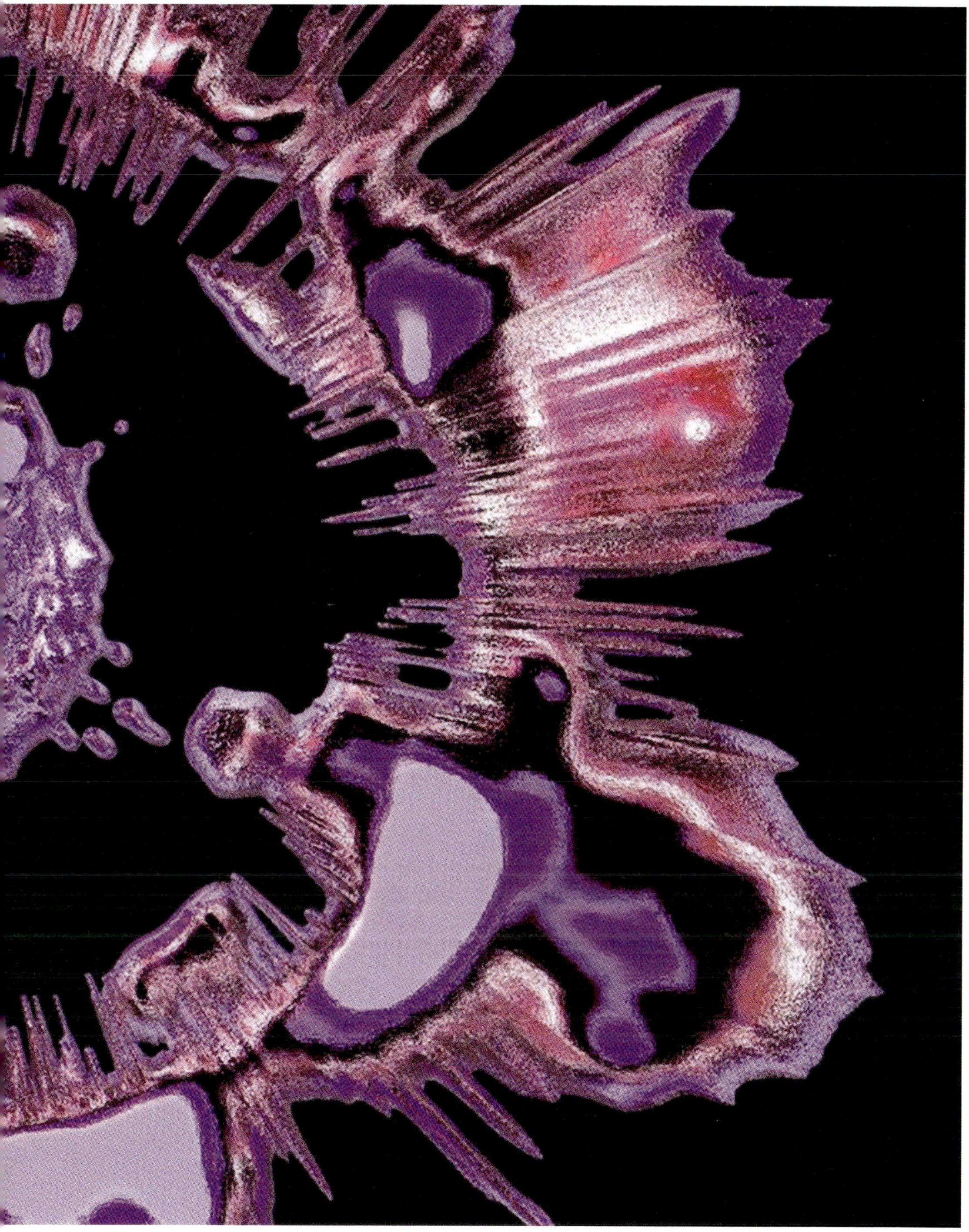

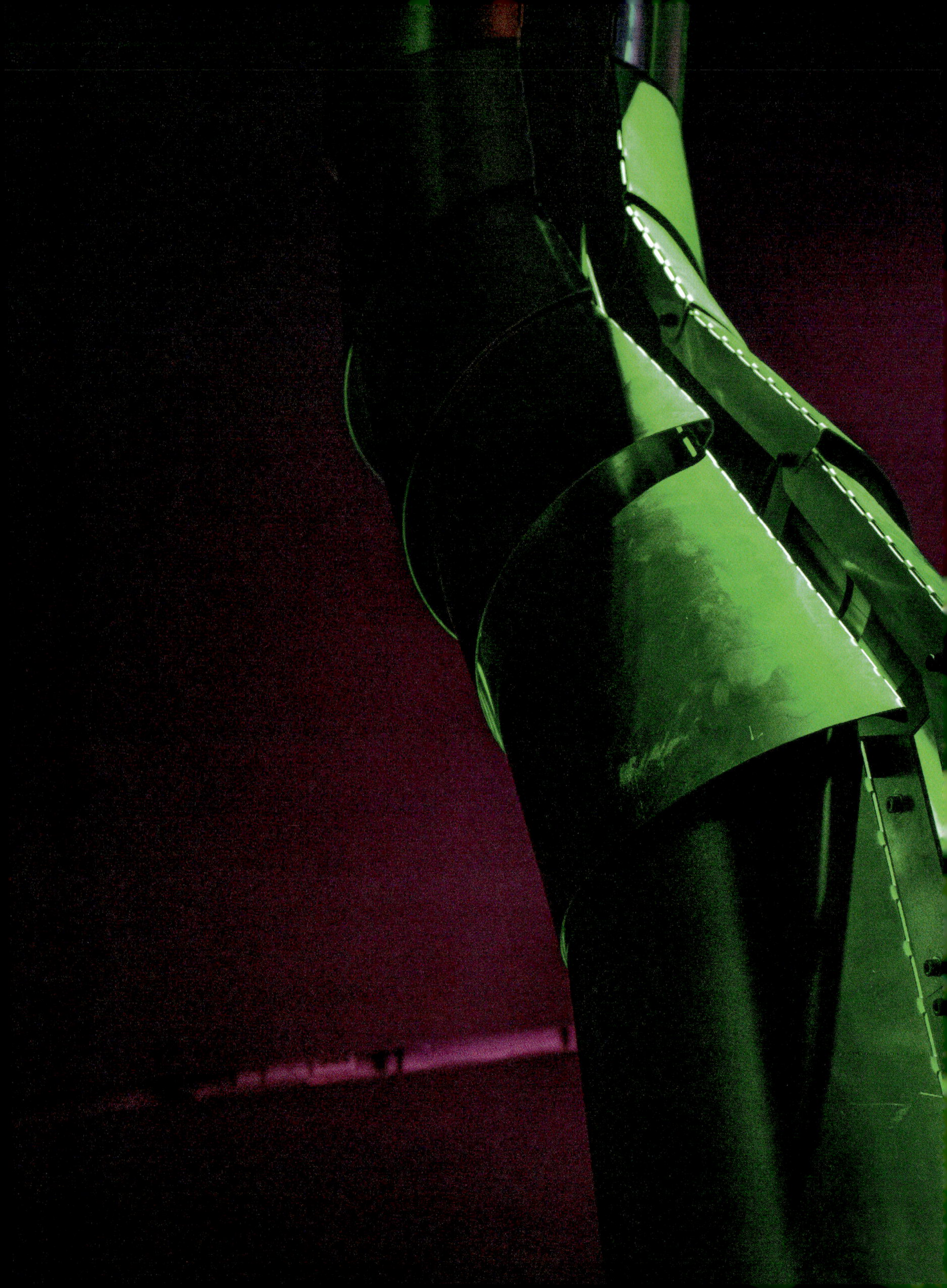

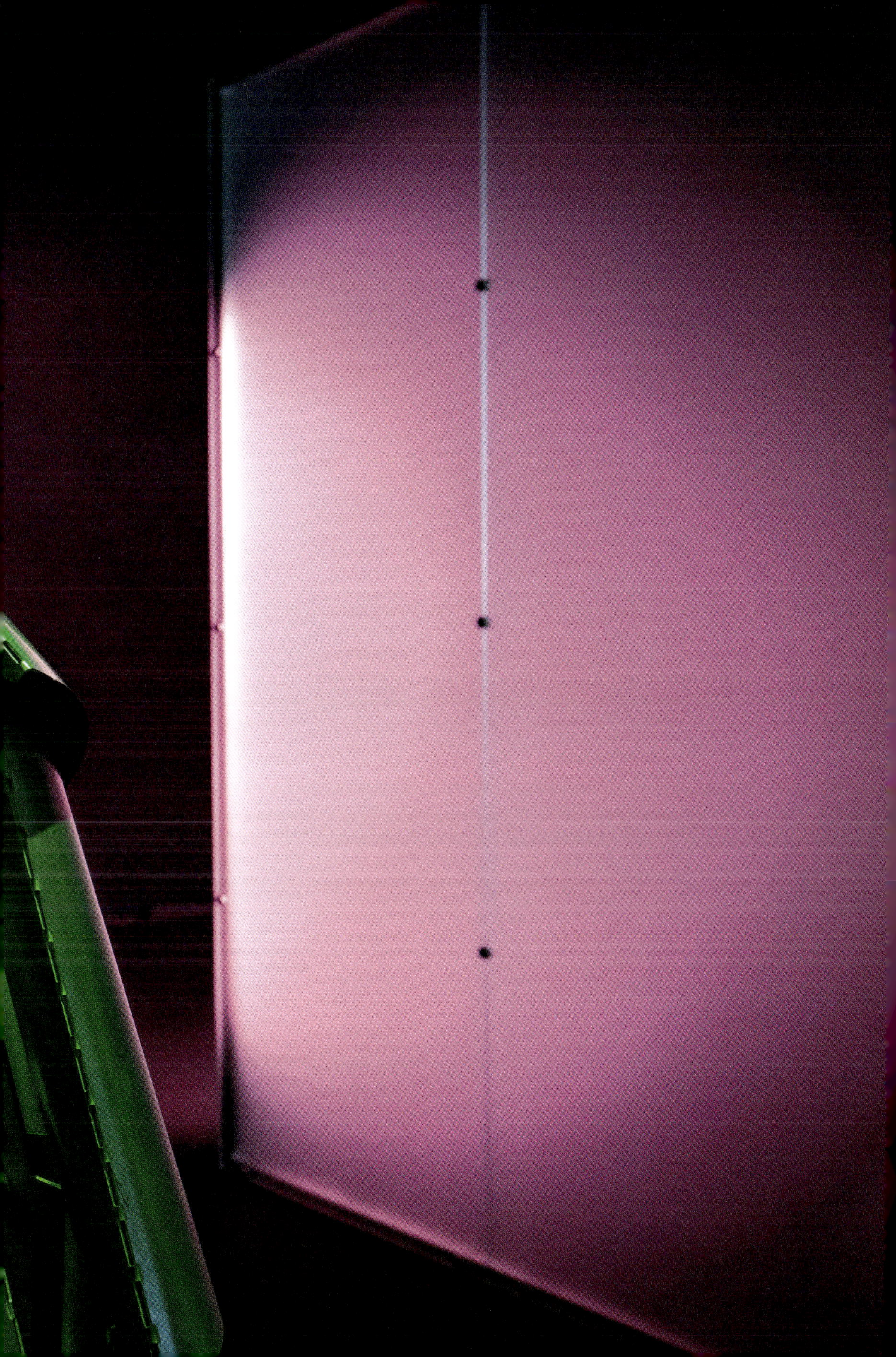

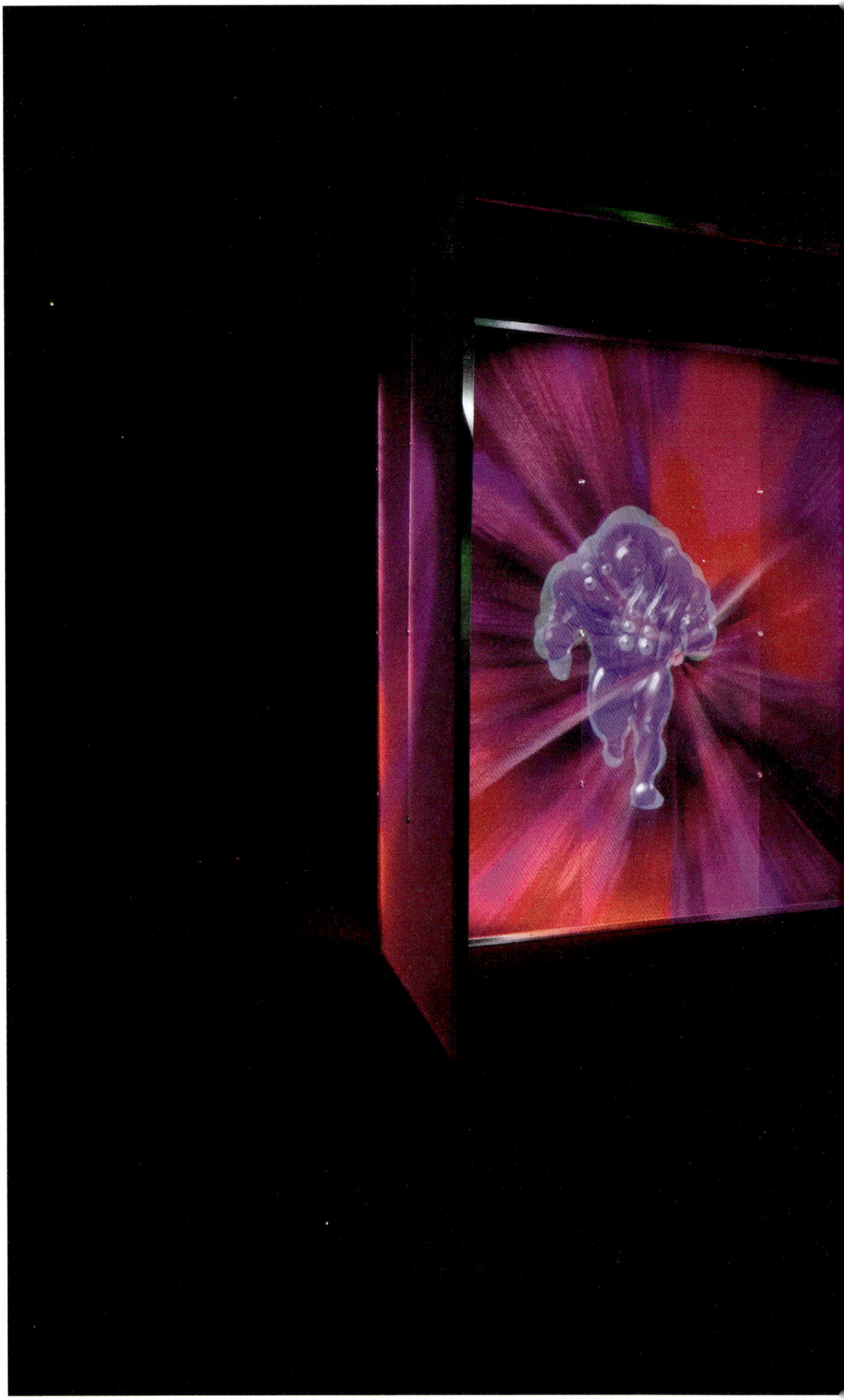

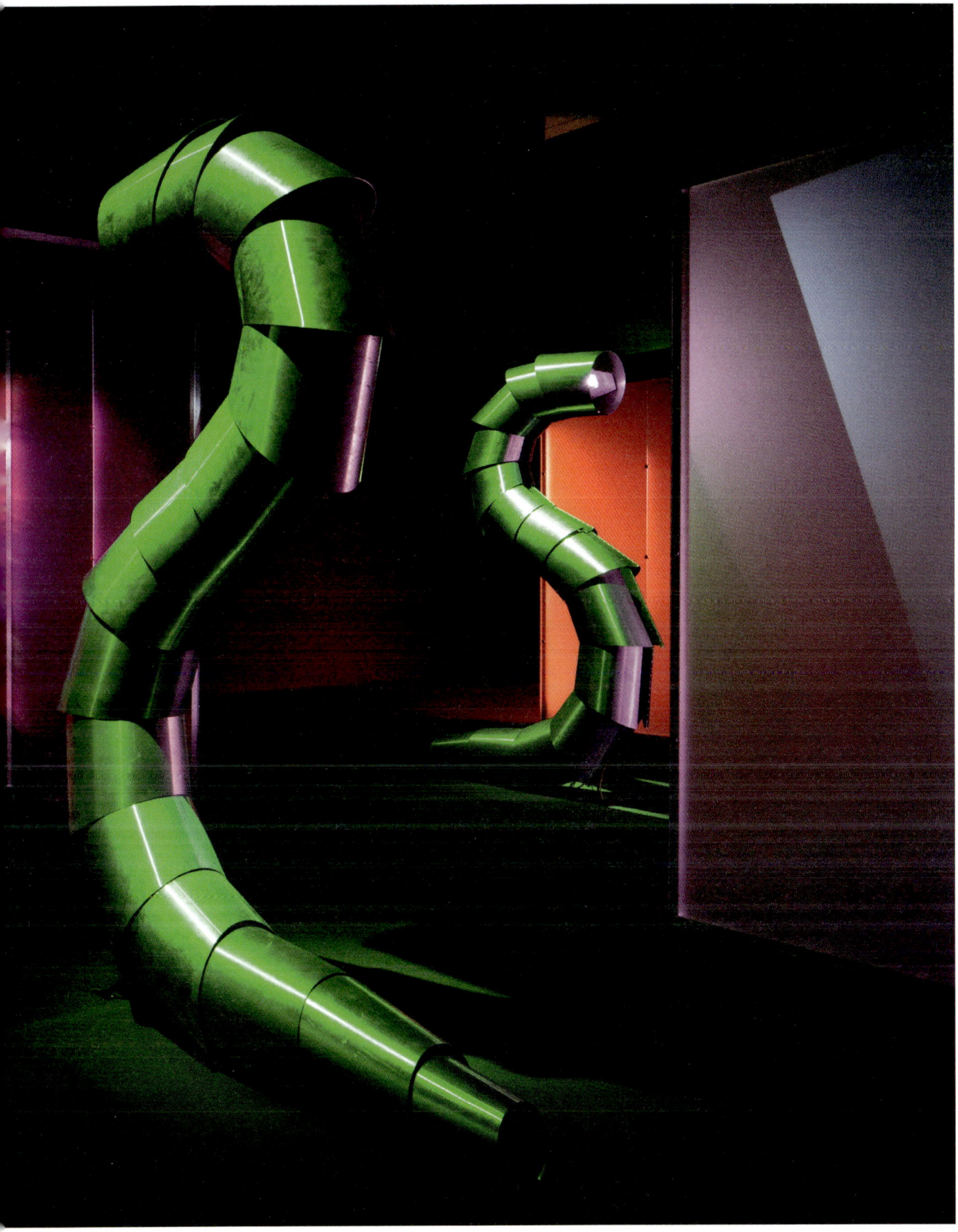

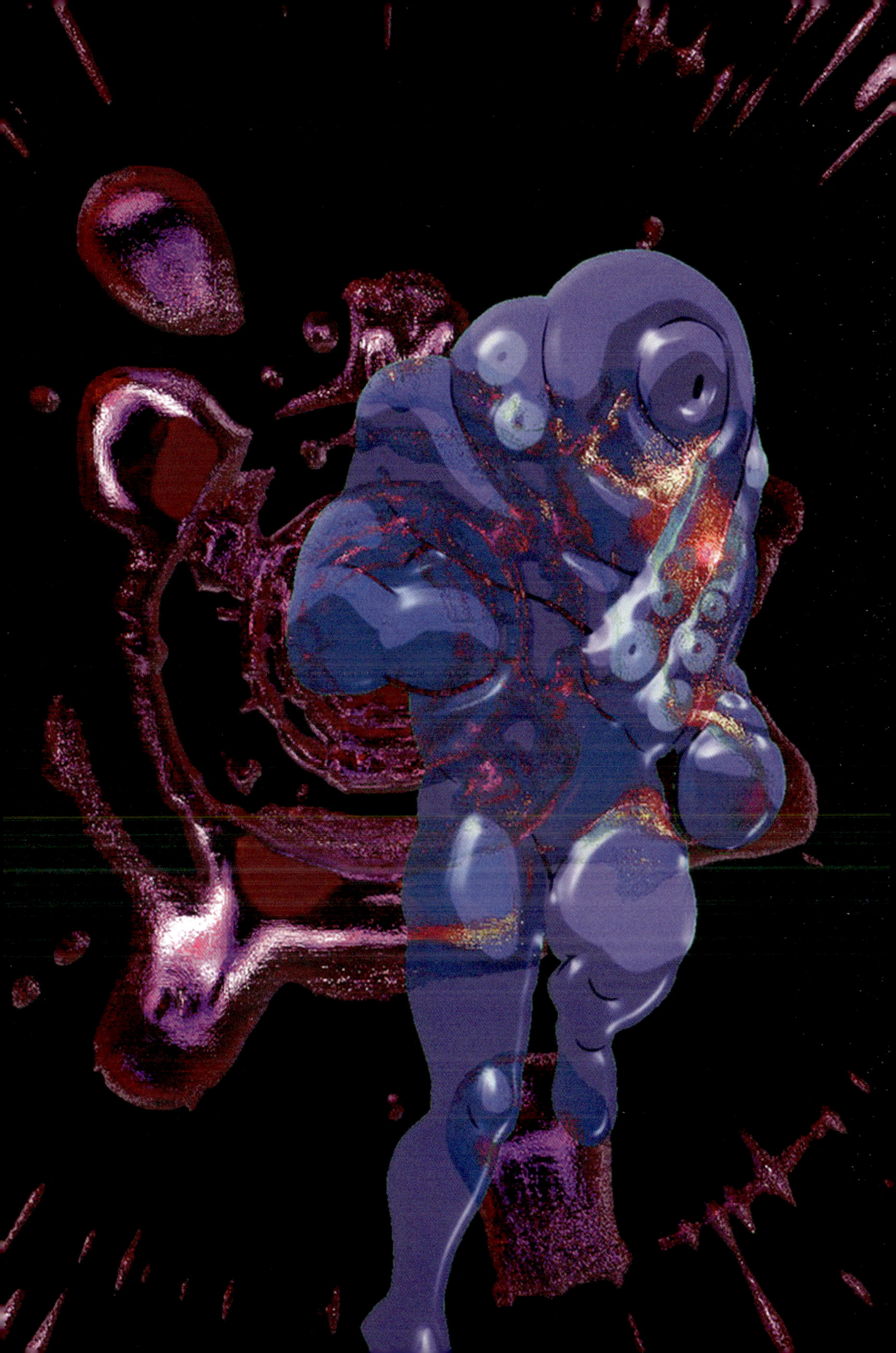

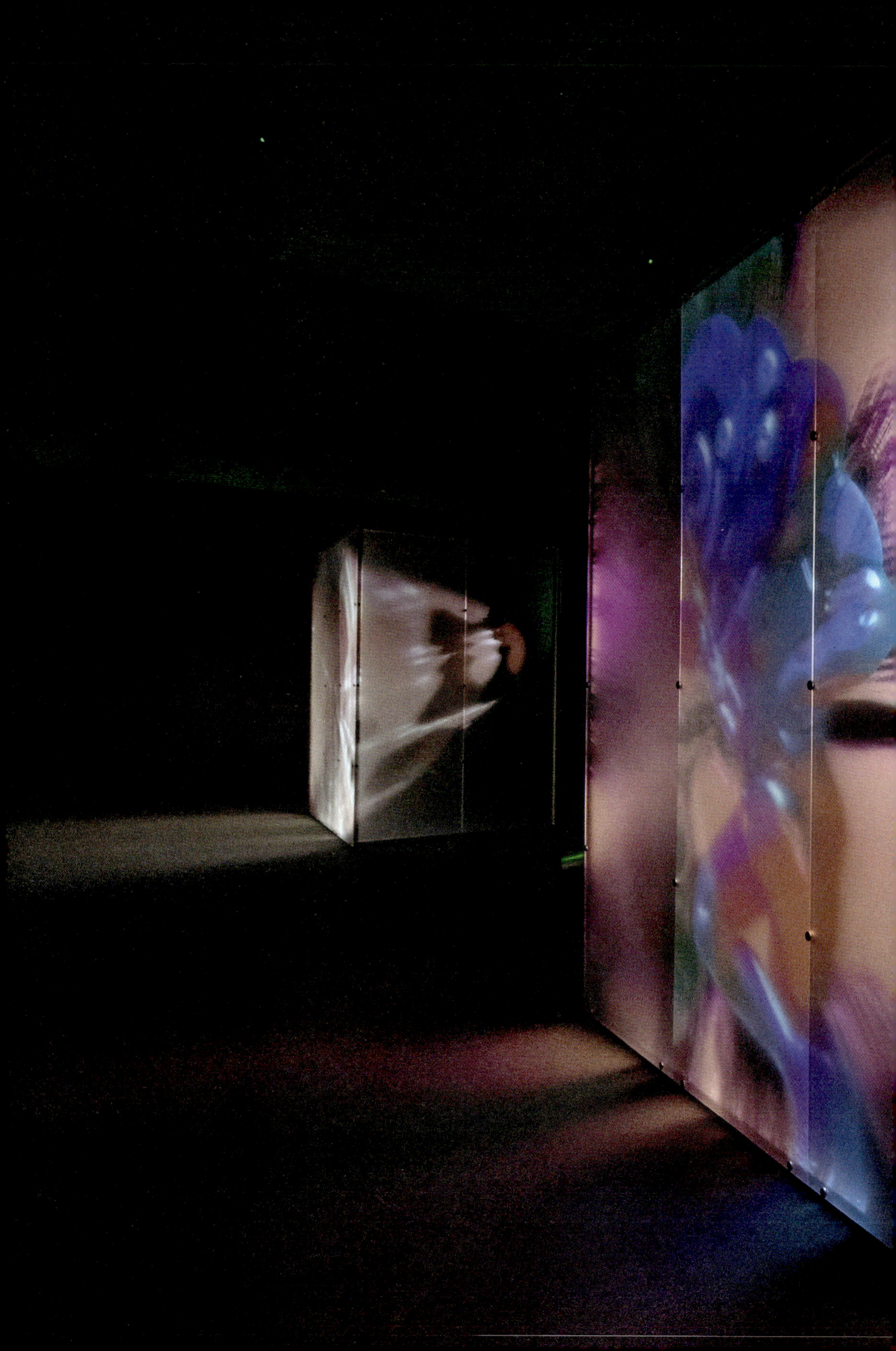

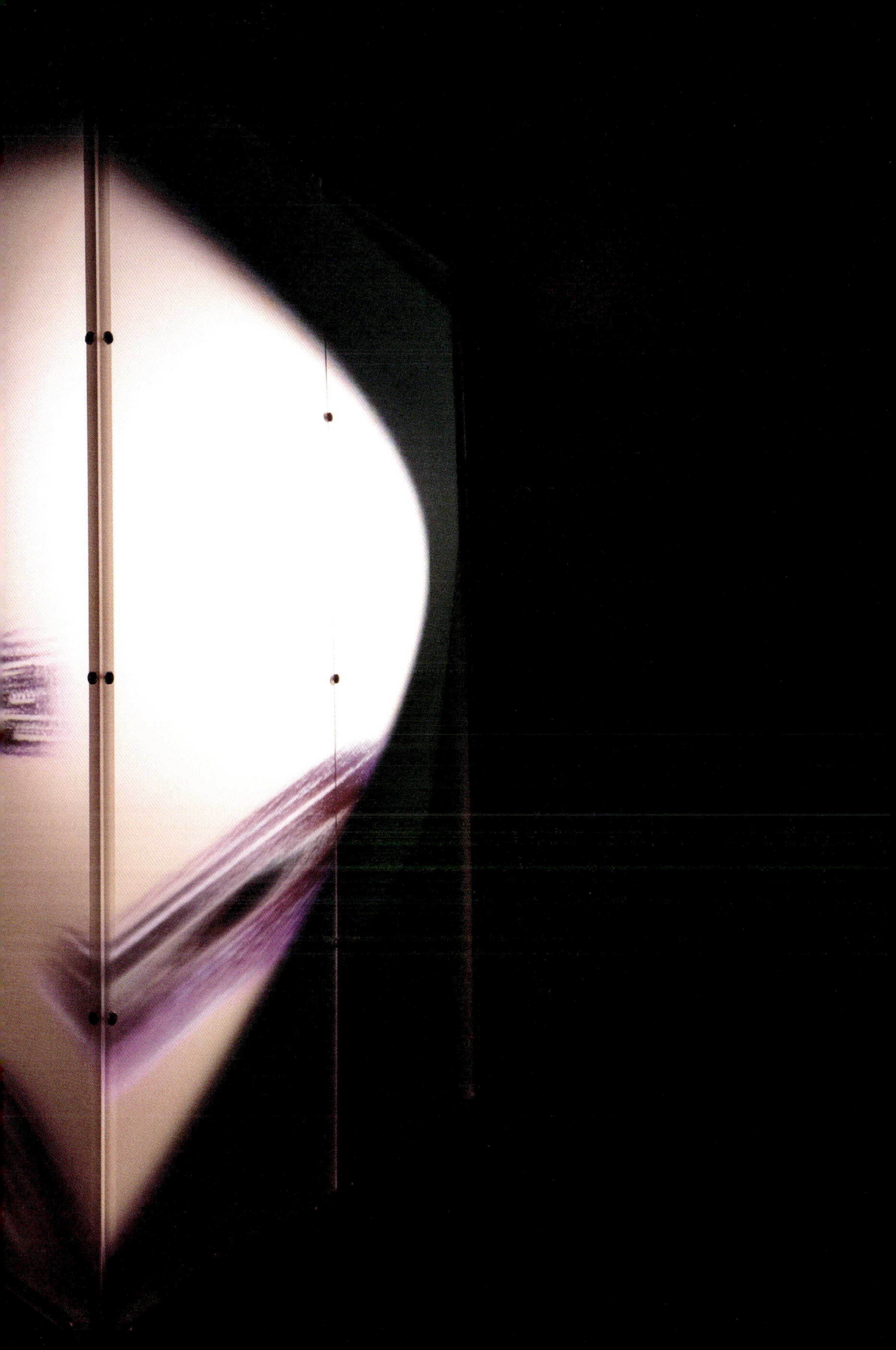

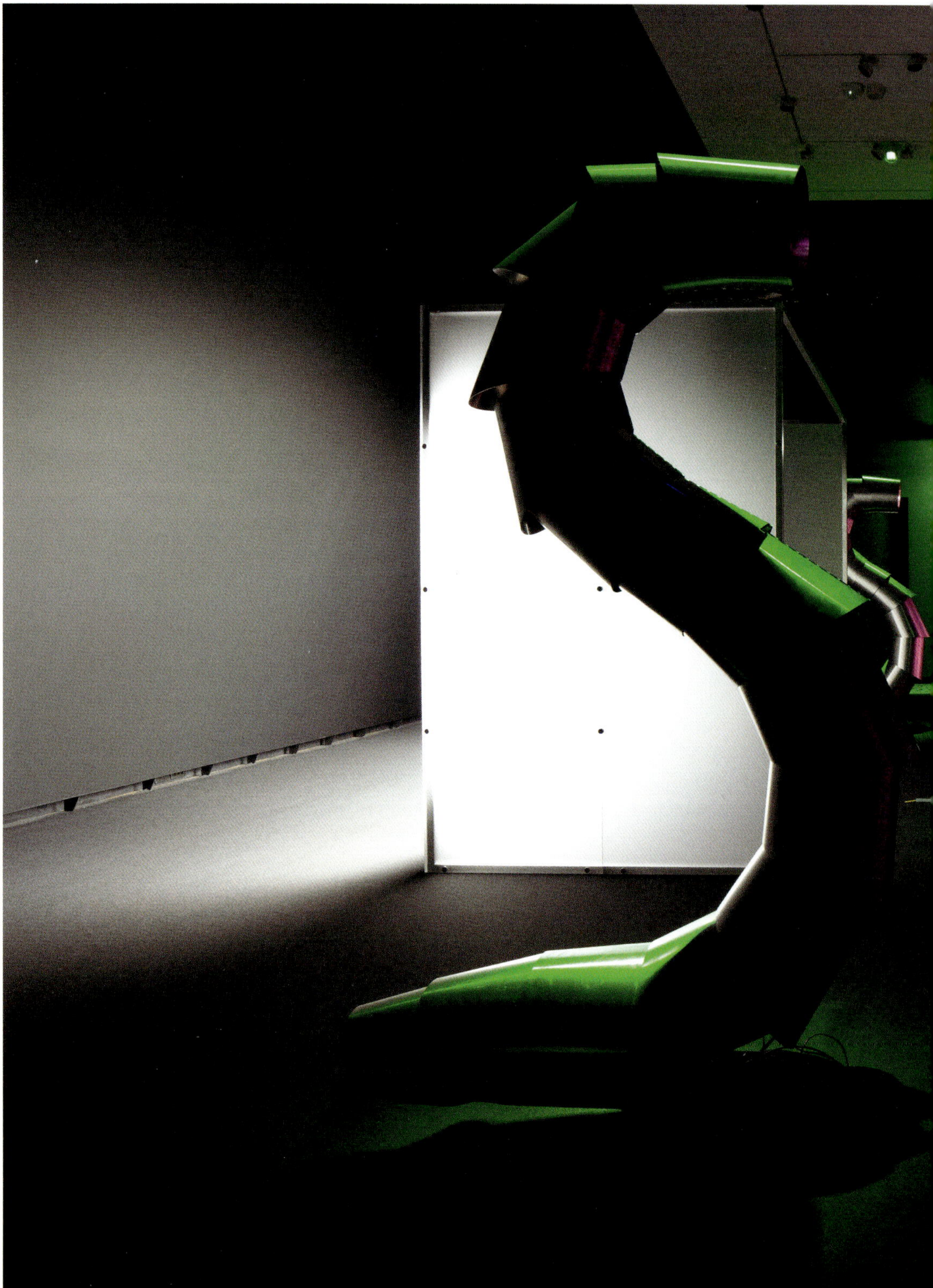

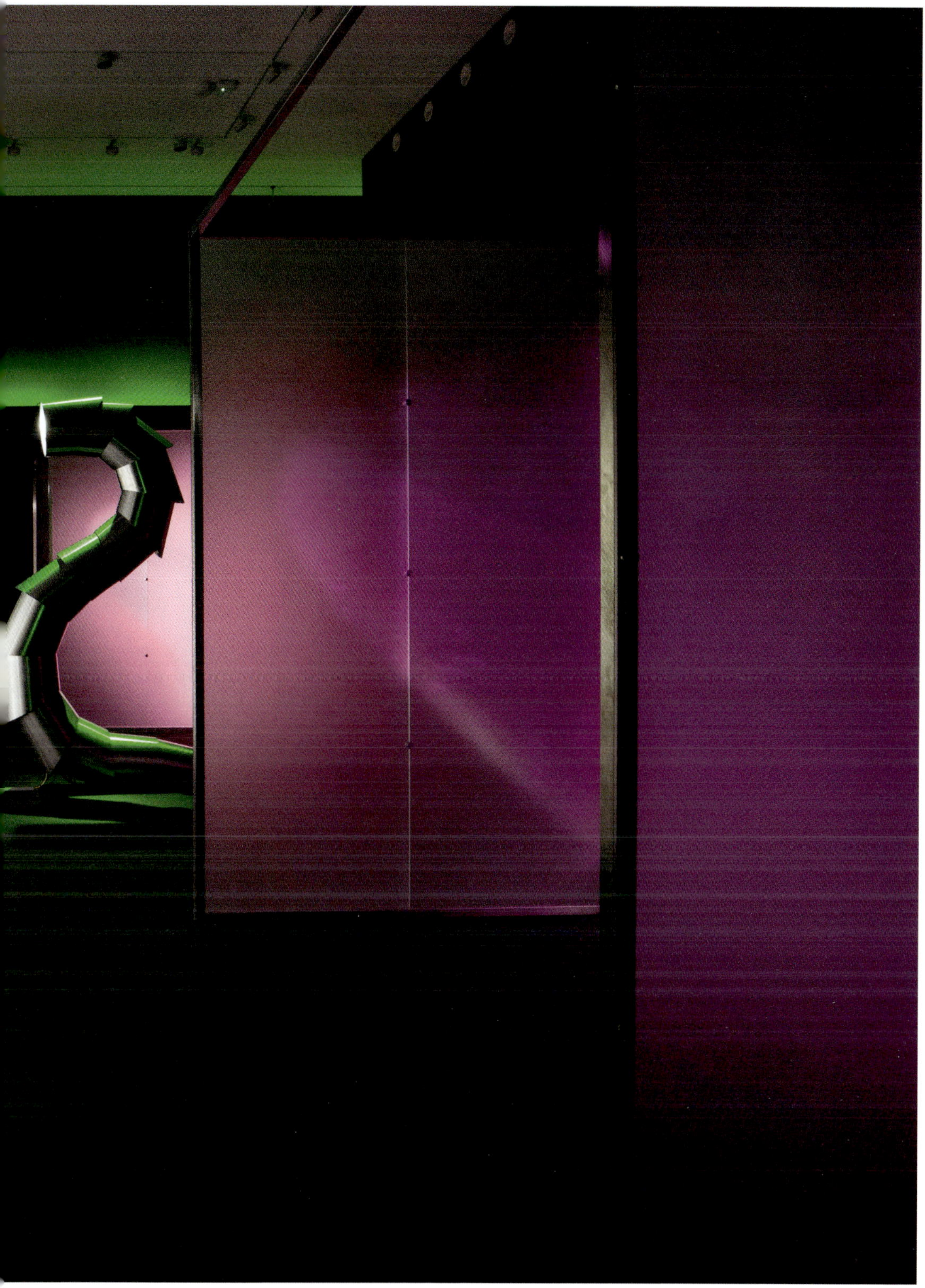

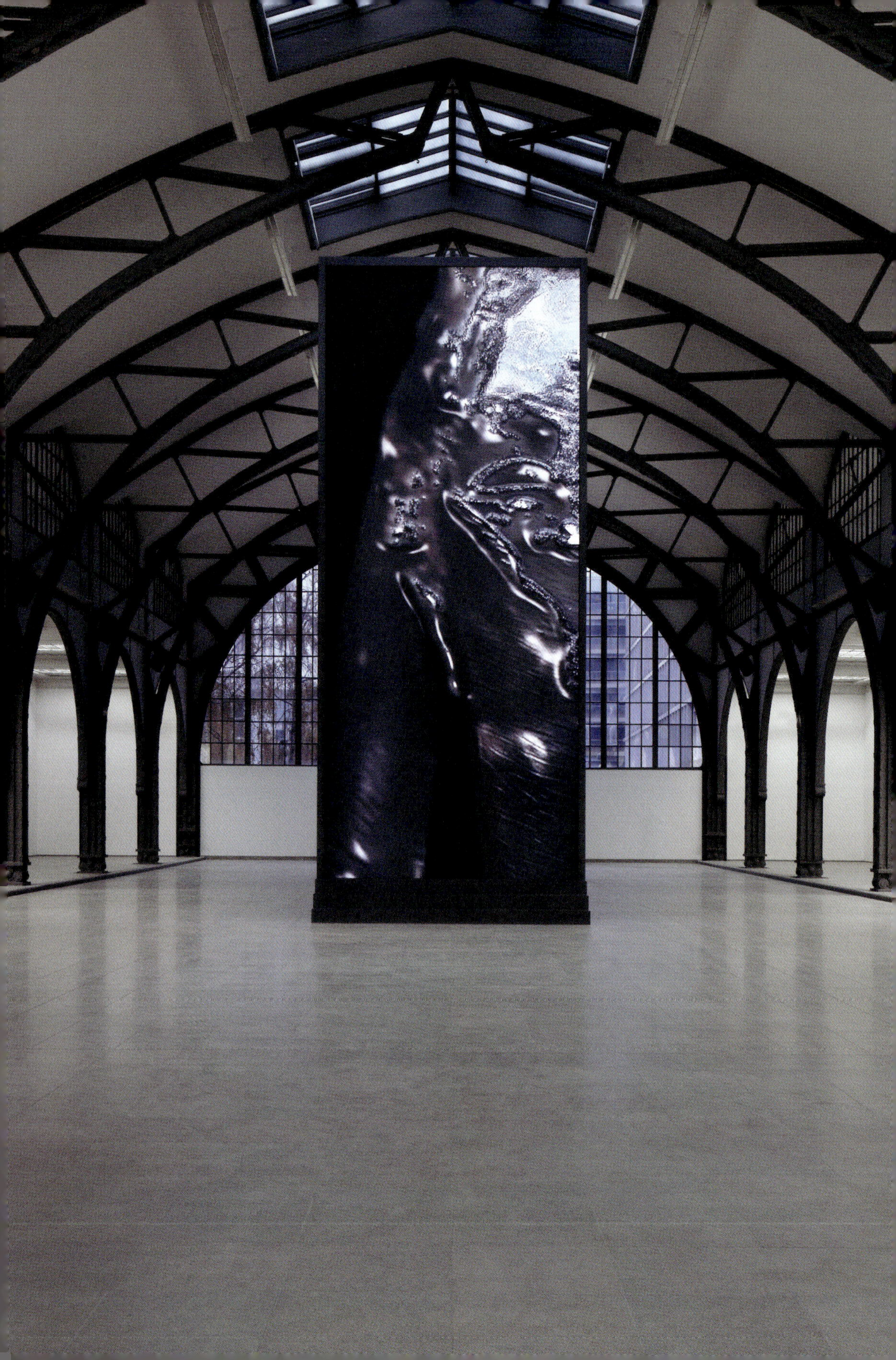

Nijah Cunningham

AFTER, AFTER THE END OF THE WORLD— SANDRA MUJINGA'S ART OF ENTANGLEMENT

A dark, narrow corridor opens on to a sparsely lit room containing three video sculptures, each featuring a metallic snake-like creature that projects colorful digital animations onto semi-transparent Plexiglas cubicles to the accompaniment of an ambient soundtrack. This is the "shadow world"° that visitors encounter in *Closed Space, Open World* (2022) by Congolese–Norwegian musician, video, and installation artist Sandra Mujinga. The inaugural exhibition commissioned as part of the emerging artists series *SOLO OSLO* at MUNCH, Mujinga's installation creates an immersive experience in which visitors are invited to linger with the strange and unfamiliar, the alien and unknown, the monstrous and fantastic, and inhabit the wonderous and frightful expanse of enclosure.

Timotheus Vermeulen, "Critic's Picks: Sandra Mujinga, Munch Museet, January 22, 2022—April 3, 2022" *Artforum.* https://www.artforum.com/events/sandra-mujinga-249696/

Mujinga's art is an inhabitation of the more-or-less, of the interstitial extraterrestriality of refuge found at the convergence of refuse and refusal.° "This cosmos (in the proper sense of the word) is as familiar as it is disorienting, both enthralling and distressing," writes art critic Timotheus Vermeulen about the MUNCH exhibition.° Those familiar with the writings of Frantz Fanon might recall a similar push and pull, recoil and allure, in the psychiatrist and anticolonial thinker's attitude toward the "atmosphere of myths and magic" that envelops the colonized subject.° A retreat to the world of fantasy and superstition was viewed by Fanon as a pathological response to colonial oppression. The native finds compensation for the humiliation and subjugation experienced under colonial rule in "a permanent confrontation at the level of phantasy."° For Fanon, anticolonial struggle results when "victims of unspeakable terrors" once content with losing themselves in "hallucinatory dreams"

Fred Moten, "Notes on Passage (The New International of Sovereign Feelings)," *Palimpsest: A Journal on Women, Gender, and the Black International* 3, no. 1 (2014): 67.

Vermeulen, "Critic's Picks: Sandra Mujinga."

Frantz Fanon, *The Wretched of the Earth*, trans., Richard Philcox (1963; repr., New York: Grove Press, 2004), 18.

Ibid., 19.

Ibid

are driven to political action and leave the world of shadows behind.° I bring up Fanon's formulation of this extra-political terrain to draw attention to the critical intervention that Mujinga's art both embodies and puts forth. Thinking about inhabitation in relation to her sculptures, performances, videos, and installations enables the acknowledgement of the theoretical practice her work facilitates. What we encounter in Mujinga's work is not some uncritical valorization of the forms of cultural resistance harbored in the world of the occult but the demonstration of a receptive attitude toward precisely what Fanon regards as a "zone of nonbeing" that she cultivates through her artistic practice.°

Frantz Fanon, *Black Skin, White Masks,* trans. Richard Philcox (1952; repr., New York: Grove Press, 2008), xii.

Working at the convergence of speculative fiction, black study, and posthumanism, Mujinga often describes her artistic practice as drawing on the tradition of Afro-futurism while, less frequently, engaging with the school of thought called Afropessimism. In reference to her performance work, *You Are All You Need* (2019), where two artists are caught in an exchange in the aftermath of a seismic event, she underlines the importance to "pursue practices and engage in discussions—as Afropessimism reminded me—that do not have solutions." ° Her disavowal of teleological narratives of overcoming is inspired by a theory of anti-blackness put forth by the likes of Frank Wilderson III and Jared Sexton which argues that there is a fundamental antagonism between blackness and civil society that is constitutive of the world as such.° If the onto-epistemological ground of being is predicated on the negation of blackness, as the theory goes, then, anything short of the radical upheaval of the world as such simply reproduces the fundamental logic of anti-blackness. And yet,

Eric Otieno Sumba, "Sandra Mujinga's Spectral Figures Evoke Dark Histories and a Murky Present," *Frieze* (March 23, 2021). https://www.frieze.com/ko/article/sandra-mujinga-spectral-figures-2021

See Frank Wilderson III, *Red, White, and Black: Cinema and the Structure of U.S. Antagonisms* (Durham, NC: Duke University Press, 2010).

what we encounter in Mujinga's art might be better described as a reformulation or even a critique of the thesis of ontological negation that these thinkers inherit and embrace from Fanon's concept of nonbeing. In an interview with curator and writer Legacy Russell on the occasion of the 2021 New Museum Triennial, Mujinga gestures towards something like a post-pessimist horizon in which "nonbeing" is given over as a sort of superposition when she states, "Blackness can host many things at the same time." ° To be host to many things *at the same time* describes a radical simultaneity that entails nothing short of an enfolding of time and space that collapses the distinction between here and there, then and now. Quantum physics invites us to inhabit, if only hypothetically, the perspective of an electron or some "flying particle wander[ing] the darkness" as a way of troubling classical metaphysics' imagining of being and nonbeing as discrete states.° Modernity is the production and reproduction of statelessness in the name of a tyrannical entity that is the sovereign subject. The thing is that statelessness is not some opposing state just like how nonbeing is not the opposite of being. In both cases, the apparent negation of a state of being results not in nothingness but discloses a complex dynamic field of relationality. It is in that field that we discover the rich theoretical practice that is Mujinga's art of entanglement.

Before going any further, I must say that I came late to Afro-futurism. It is only recently that I have begun to embrace the conceptual resources that science fiction offers for addressing the problems that black being poses to modern thought. Fortunately, Mujinga's work has received its due attention from art critics more versed in the topic. Others have already detailed her deployment of

"Sandra Mujinga and Legacy Russell," in Margot Norton and Jamillah James, eds., *Soft Water Hard Stone: 2021 New Museum Triennial* (New York: Phaidon, 2021), 302. Drawing on the famous Schrödinger's cat experiment, Karen Barad describes superposition as undoing assumptions concerning the nature of being and time: "Quantum superpositions radically undo classical notions of identity and being... Quantum superpositions (at least on [Niels] Bohr's account) tell us that being/becoming is an indeterminate matter: there simply *is not a determinate fact of the matter* concerning the cat's state of being alive or dead." Karen Barad, "Quantum Entanglements and Hauntological Relations of Inheritance: Dis/continuities, SpaceTime Enfoldings, and Justice-to-Come," *Derrida Today* 3, no. 2 (2010): 251, original emphasis. We need to at least acknowledge the incompatibility of quantum mechanics and theory of general relativity and their respective concerns with probability and gravity as the warping of space-time. See the research of Jonathan Oppenheim at University College of London.

Michael Frayn, *Copenhagen* (New York: Anchor Books, 2000), 88 quoted in Barad, "Quantum Entanglements and Hauntological Relations of Inheritance," 242.

strategies of worldbuilding specific to the genre of science fiction. Others have already identified the resonances between the speculative worlds that her wearable sculptures, performance-based works, video, and multimedia installations make imaginable and the literary innovations of the likes of Octavia Butler, Samuel Delany, and Ursula le Guin. Others have already commented on how the hybrid figures that populate Mujinga's sound and video installations traverse the boundary between the human and nonhuman. Others have already talked about how her approach to art making amounts to a series of "ongoing experiments in how to exist as a subject in a hyper-mediated world."° Altogether, Mujinga's work continues to inspire deeply stimulating criticism that interrogates how the category of the human functions as a technology of power that perpetuates the racial, global capitalist order under which we live.

Kiki Mazzucchelli, "Future Greats: Sandra Mujinga," ArtReview (April 17, 2017). https://artreview.com/jan-feb-2017-future-great-sandra-mujinga/

Closed Space, Open World is an incredible manifestation of the speculative realities that Mujinga creates in the name of Afro-futurism. Made in collaboration with artist Saphira Nancy, the animation projected on the frosted Plexiglas cubicles features an avatar that runs across three screens and morphs between human and non-human forms. What initially appear as long tentacles spewing from an orifice soon resemble dreadlocks once the avatar reveals its humanoid head from under a purple garment or flesh. This is against the backdrop of animated sequences that recall music visualization and, as Vermeulen observes, are suggestive of "perspectival movement...as if the immobilized viewer were traveling through space at warp speed."° The Plexiglas surfaces serve as portals that are activated from inside of the giant serpentine figures

Timotheus Vermeulen, "Critic's Picks: Sandra Mujinga."

encased in aluminum and drenched in a green light. Here, the humanoid is born out of an inner vision of the non-human form that, in itself, blurs the distinction between technology and organic life. What if this thing we call the "human" is destined to be nothing more than a future memory? What form will the human take when remembered in a posthuman future? What does this process of becoming-memory portend for the fate of humanity? What possibilities for the here and now come into view from the perspective of a memory foretold? Despite my somewhat belated encounter with Afro-futurism, I, like many, am familiar with the refrain featured on the live album recorded by Sun Ra and His Intergalactic Research Arkestra at the Donaueschingen and Berlin Festivals in 1970: "It's after the end of the world. Don't you know that yet?"° A brilliant formulation of Afro-futurist sensibility, what one also hears in this refrain is a revisioning of a prevailing worldview in the 1970s that challenges the narration of the ongoing destruction of human and non-human lifeworlds as a story of progress. When I hear "It's after the end of the world. Don't you know that yet?" it is impossible not to recall snippets of Gil Scott-Heron's "Whitey on the Moon" also recorded in 1970 on his album *Small Talk at 125th and Lenox:* "A rat done bit my sister Nell/ with whitey on the moon." ° If I was ever hesitant to embrace Afro-futurism it was out of a concern with the law of genre that determines the shape of the tradition. Often, examples of Afro-futurism emerge against a muted backdrop and severed from sociality. Small talk, chatter, rumor, and conspiracy are dimensions of everyday life that remain ensnared in the same "atmosphere of myths and magic" that Fanon recoils from. The challenge with Fanon's concept of nonbeing is that in the effort to illustrate

Sun Ra and His Intergalactic Research Arkestra, *It's After the End of The World — Live At The Donaueschingen And Berlin Festivals* (MPS 1970).

Gil Scott-Heron, *A New Black Poet: Small Talk at 125th and Lenox* (Flying Dutchman 1970).

the ontological negation that anti-black, colonial violence carries out, he must disregard the means through which those deemed insignificant and expendable routinely make meaning of their own disposability. Spooky realms emerge that are devoid of any political significance and are seen by Fanon as the psychopathological effects of racialized violence. Fanon probably did not have science fiction or Afro-futurism in mind when he developed his thesis of ontological negation and we can never know if he would see any resemblance between the speculative realities Mujinga conjures and life in the bush of ghosts. We do know that Mujinga is uniquely attuned to the muted backdrop of anticolonial politics that Fanon would likely explain away as background noise. In fact, if you really listen to the ambient soundtrack that accompanies *Closed Space, Open World* and many of Mujinga's other works you can hear a subtle refusal of nonbeing. Here, she cxplains how she works with sound:

> When I start producing a soundtrack, I often envision a body with a specific heartbeat—whether it resembles a whale's heartbeat, which can range from two to ten beats per minute, an elephant's, at 25 to 30 beats per minute, or our own, at 60 to 100 beats per minute. The soundtrack becomes an anchor, providing a sense of rhythm and time. °

Tendai John Mutambu, "Sandra Mujinga: 'I felt a very urgent need to gather people,'" *Ocula Magazine* (November 19, 2024). https://ocula.com/magazine/conversations/sandra-mujinga-on-the-power-of-the-voice/

One can never be certain whether the ambient sounds in Mujinga's work emanate from some far-off form of existence or are the synchronized expression of an immense vital system that already envelopes her speculative worlds. Both Gil Scott-Heron's small talk and the murmurings of a vitality that Mujinga produces invite serious consideration of the immanence that ambience harbors. "The world has ended so many times, again and again," Mujinga tells Russell, articulating what amounts to a brilliant re-reading of the Afro-futurist refrain provided by Sun Ra and His Intergalactic Research Arkestra. To bear the knowledge of that "again and again," of the recursive motion of an ending that knows no end, is to demonstrate an awareness of the *aftermaths* of Afro-futurism and what it means to be living after, *after* the end of the world. Again and again, the end of the world recalls its prior destruction and anticipates coming disasters. Rather than a linear progression, time moves as a serial upheaval in Mujinga's art. Echoes of black sociality or a reverberation from the deep, Mujinga avails us to the barely audible traces of lifeworlds that we can neither grasp nor outright deny. This spooky element of her work speaks to her unique attitude and attunement to zones of nonbeing and the void.

Spooky things occur after, after the end of the world. The most inconspicuous object is densely animated with longings and desires. "When I see second-hand garments or just a jacket on the floor somewhere, I think about the body that's no longer there." ° *Spectral Keepers* (2020), the sprawling installation that was the first work visitors encountered at the base of the rotunda of the Guggenheim Museum during the 2023 exhibition *Going Dark*, features cone-like baskets that lay at the feet of Mujinga's 9 foot tall figures. These objects resemble the huge wicker fishing baskets developed over generations in the Wagenia Falls region of the Democratic Republic of Congo. If technology can be defined as a mode of unconcealment and not simply an extension of human activity, the fishing baskets in *Spectral Keepers* are suggestive of emergent lifeworlds from

Mujinga and Russell, *Soft Water Hard Stone*, 301.

which they were severed prior to materializing in this otherworldly context. Mujinga's discussion of the work *IBMSWR: I Build My Skin with Rocks* (2022) further articulates the temporal entanglements of living after, after the end of the world:

> I sometimes like to write a text before I make sculptures or work in different mediums. I did that for *IBMSWR*: I wrote about a mutated elephant-human, being the last of her kind, living in a dark industrial world. I was thinking a lot about my grandmother, who I never really got to know. She became this character I could write about, and later, I speculated whether she was my grandmother or my future self. This figure moved through the world, bearing witness to all these histories, having to continue living to tell the stories about what she had heard and seen.[°]

Mutambu, "Sandra Mujinga."

A similar entanglement of past, present, and future, is produced in *Closed Space, Open World* through the patterns of recurrence that emerge between it and other works. The light that drenches the snake-like creatures is of the same hue of chroma green as the light that saturates works such as *Nocturnal Kinship* (2018), *SONW—Shadow of New World* (2019), *Spectral Keepers* (2020), *Reworlding Remains* (2021), and *Grief* (2024). This is while the avatar's tentacles/dreadlocks recall the faux leather wall sculptures in *And What Was Left* (2023) that hang like hunting trophies. The back ends of the giant aluminum snake-like creatures also appear in *Love Language* (2023) where they are seen burrowing in different directions through the walls of the gallery space. However, the three-channel video installation, *Pervasive Light* (2021), where a shadowy figure appears and disappears across the screens stationed in a dark room, is among the most jarring manifestations of Mujinga's art of entanglement. Darkness is given over as non-locality. After immersing oneself in the work, there is a brief moment of uncertainty when exiting the dark room when it is unclear whether one will show up in the Upper East Side of Manhattan or Berlin or Copenhagen or some other place and time altogether.

As visitors make their way to *Closed Space, Open World*, they must pass through a narrow corridor with an one-way glass panel installed into the wall. Made popular by interrogation scenes dramatized in police procedurals, this subtle element in the installation speaks to Mujinga's extended engagement with themes of surveillance and capture. Usually, the one-way glass appears reflective on one side and transparent on the other. While standing in a dark room, one can look onto the well-lit room on the other side of the glass undetected. From the very outset of *Closed Space, Open World*, the glass panel produces a strange sense that one is being watched from the other side. But within the dark corridor one cannot tell on what side one resides. It is unclear who is watching and who is being watched. One is unsure whether there is an imperceptible presence looking in from the other side, the darker side of the glass. If the frosted Plexiglas cubicles in the main room of the installation act as portals, one wonders if the one-way glass opens onto a similar folding of the space-time continuum. Before entering the main room, before approaching the imposing metallic creatures drenched in green light, before witnessing the posthuman avatar figure flitting across the Plexiglas surfaces, visitors are already made to traverse the edge of an expanse found in enclosure. Again, push and pull. The darkness of Mujinga's shadow worlds is the non-local site of a dynamic "intra-action" in which the eerie sensation of being watched by some imperceptible presence is impossible to distinguish from the gravitational pull of something akin to dark matter.° After, after the end of the world, Mujinga shows us how the genuine inhabitation of aftermaths demands nothing less than "touching upon the void."°

"In contrast to the usual 'interaction,'" Barad explains, "the notion of *intra-action* recognises that distinct entities, agencies, events do not precede, but rather emerge from/through their intra-action." Barad, "Quantum Entanglements and Hauntological Relations of Inheritance," fn. 1, 267.

Mujinga and Russell, *Soft Water Hard Stone*, 302.

IMPRINT

This catalouge is published in
conjuction with the exhibition

SANDRA MUJINGA
CLOSED SPACE,
OPEN WORLD

SOLO OSLO
MUNCH
22.01.22-03.04.22

Publication

Editor:
Therese Möllenhoff,
Canica

Project Manager:
Monica Borg Fure,
Talent Norway

Design:
Anette L'orange,
Blunderbuss

Edition: 700
Printed by:
Livonia Print

ISBN 978–82–8462–049–7

Paper: Arctic Volume White 130 gsm
Typesetting:
Neue Haas Unica
Garamond Premiere Pro

ACKNOWLEDGMENTS

Art Project
Artist: Sandra Mujinga
2D-animation: Saphira Nancy

MUNCH Team
Curator: Tominga O'Donnell
Concept developer: Tove Aadland Sørvåg
Project Manager: Gisle Sandvand
Text Editor: Hanna Hille Stoltenberg
Registrar: Tine Schmidt Haislund
Head of Marketing: Tone Brunner
Technical Producer:
Fredrik Wold-Hansen
Exhibiton Technician:
Tor-Björn Adlegren
Art Technician Management:
Timothy Brignall
Art Technician:
Tomas Siqveland Einarsson
Art Technician: Jessica MacMillan
Exhibition Architect: Kolab Arkitekter
Light Design: Tara Fox
AV technician:
Karl Richard Alexandersson

SOLO OSLO Mediation Project
Mediator: Zeenat Amiri

Thanks to Dr. Henza Anwar,
Begard Reza and and Hamda Barise
from Salam, a non-profit organization
that supports LGBTQ+ people
from Muslim backgrounds.

SOLO OSLO is an exhibition series at MUNCH presented with support from Talent Norway and Canica. *SOLO OSLO* contributes to developing the local art scene by giving Oslo-based, newly established artists an opportunity to develop their practice through a solo exhibition at the museum.

Talent Norway is an initiative aiming at helping young artists advance further within their field, founded by Sparebankstiftelsen DNB, Cultiva and the Norwegian Ministry of Culture. *SOLO OSLO* one of the visual art programs in the portfolio of Talent Norway.

Canica is the family company of Stein Erik Hagen and a proud supporter of MUNCH. The Canica Art Collection collaborates with museums worldwide and artworks from the collection are on long term loan to several museum collections, including MUNCH, Oslo; KODE Art Museums, Bergen; The National Gallery of Denmark, Copenhagen and the van Gogh Museum, Amsterdam.

MUNCH Talent Norge canica